Cookery Activities

Lynne Burgess

Bright Ideas
for Early Years

Published by Scholastic Publications Ltd,
Villiers House, Clarendon Avenue,
Leamington Spa, Warwickshire CV32 5PR

© 1995 Scholastic Publications Ltd
Text © 1995 Lynne Burgess

Written by Lynne Burgess
Editor Noel Pritchard
Assistant Editor Kate Banham
Designer Tracey Ramsey
Illustrator Susan Hutchison
Photographs by Martin Sookias
Grateful thanks to the staff and pupils of
Cannon Park Primary School, Coventry, who
are featured in these photographs.
Cover design by Lynne Joesbury
Cover photograph by Martyn Chillmaid

Typeset by Typesetters (Birmingham) Ltd
Artwork by Steve Williams & Associates, Leicester

Printed at Alden Press Limited, Oxford and Northampton,
Great Britain

British Library Cataloguing in Publication Data
A catalogue record for this book is available from the British
Library

ISBN 0-590-53324-X

Contents

Introduction

Cookery is a popular activity for many early years pupils. A large number of children will already have enjoyed helping to prepare food at home but even if some children have not been involved at home, most will be keen to join in if given the opportunity.

As well as being great fun, cooking is a valuable educational experience. Many young children are already establishing strong preferences for particular foods. Cookery activities offer an opportunity to discuss nutrition and health to help children understand the advantages and disadvantages of the various food choices open to them. Food can be used to introduce children to other countries or religions (see Chapters 8 and 9) and to help them develop an awareness of the variety of cultures and a respect for others.

Nutrition

Cookery activities are one way of helping children to make healthy choices with food. Bear this in mind when choosing recipes. If all the child's cooking experiences centre around cakes and biscuits, very little will have been done to promote a healthy diet which is essential for growth and development in the early years. The table below shows the components of a healthy diet.

There are established links between the diet of young children and future health problems such as tooth decay, heart disease, cancer and obesity. Many diseases start in childhood and a badly balanced diet can become a habit which is difficult to change. The main problems are an excess of foods containing large amounts of sugar and fat and too little fibre (found in fresh fruit, vegetables, nuts, and pulses). Many children also develop a liking for highly-salted foods which are undesirable because of the possible link to high blood pressure in later life. Look for recipes which:

- contain no salt;
- contain little or no sugar (or sugar substitutes such as honey, treacle, syrup);
- contain small amounts of fat (use polyunsaturated margarine instead of butter);
- include more fresh fruit, vegetables, wholegrains, nuts and pulses.

A balanced diet contains:

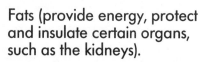

Proteins (growth and repair of body cells).

Carbohydrates (provide energy and fibre).

Fats (provide energy, protect and insulate certain organs, such as the kidneys).

Vitamins and minerals (aid growth and promote health, for example vitamin C helps cuts heal and keeps gums healthy, vitamin A helps eyes see, calcium is needed for healthy bones and teeth, iron for blood).

Water (essential for healthy functioning of all cells).

Sources

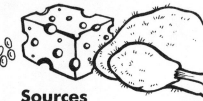

Eggs, milk, cheese, meat, fish, poultry, baked beans, lentils, pulses, fish fingers, beef burgers, nuts, seeds.

Bread, cereals, fruit, vegetables, rice, pasta, cake, jam, baked beans, sugar.

Margarine, butter, cheese, milk, cream, peanuts, chips, chocolate, meat products, oils.

Fresh and dried fruits, green salad, vegetables, meat, milk, cereals, bread, pulses, nuts, seeds.

It is tempting to play safe and only make recipes which you are sure the children will like to eat but it is important to take this opportunity to introduce them to a wide range of foods and so steer them away from an overdependence on a limited diet. As well as choosing recipes with care, adults should be aware of themselves as role models and show that they choose and enjoy 'healthy' foods.

Starting off

Start with simple recipes which contain only a few ingredients and will be quick and easy to make. Recipes with long complicated processes will be unsuitable for very young children because of their limited attention span. Once they have gained experience in simple cooking skills (chopping, stirring, whisking), then more difficult recipes can be attempted. Similarly, start with recipes for familiar food so the children feel happy and relaxed in cookery activities before introducing recipes with unusual ingredients. Always try out the recipes beforehand if you are doubtful about their suitability.

Cross-curricular links

In most early years settings, it is unlikely that the purpose of the cookery activities will be to provide the main meal of the day. It is more likely to be viewed as an educational activity which not only offers the opportunity to introduce basic home economic skills but also provides a context in which children can apply many other cross-curricular skills.

Health education

Cookery activities are an important vehicle for health education. Children are never too young to be introduced to the importance of a healthy balanced diet.

Similarly, cookery activities offer the ideal opportunity for introducing basic rules about hygiene (see page 13). A knowledge of these is essential if children are to remain healthy.

Mathematics

An amazing number of mathematical skills are embedded in cookery activities. For example, sorting activities arise naturally as children put equipment away (a set of wooden spoons) or gather ingredients (a set of apples). Cooking can involve all aspects of measuring. Compare ingredients and equipment for size (which is the largest tomato?), length (which is the longest baking tin?) and height (which is the tallest jug?). Weighing ingredients offers a chance to introduce concepts such as heavier than and lighter than as well as measuring in grams. Capacity is another important area which can be explored as children fill baking tins (full, empty) or measure liquids (litres).

Familiarity with money can be reinforced as children shop for ingredients or set up their own pretend shop (supermarket, greengrocer's, baker's). Fractions can be introduced by cutting fruit, vegetables or cakes in halves or quarters.

Encourage children to estimate as often as possible before counting or measuring.

Science

Science is another major subject which has tremendous links with cookery. As children handle ingredients they will be observing materials and describing their properties. Encourage them to use their senses throughout the cooking activity and set up smell or taste tests and 'feely' bags. Discuss the sources of the ingredients so that children begin to make links between food and plants and animals. Whenever possible, grow food to use in the cookery activities so that children can be introduced to the conditions necessary for cultivating plants.

Many recipes involve heating and cooling and this offers a chance to draw children's attention to the way things melt, solidify and change permanently as well as helping them distinguish between hot and cold. Throughout all cookery activities children should be invited to ask questions and predict possible outcomes.

English

Inevitably, many aspects of English will be reinforced through cookery activities. Speaking and listening skills will be developed as children talk about what they are doing and respond to instructions. Extend their vocabulary by always using the correct names or terms for equipment, ingredients or methods. This can be further reinforced by encouraging cookery based role-play in the home corner.

Various reading skills will be extended throughout the cookery activities. With very young children, emphasise that you are reading the recipe for instructions so they learn to associate reading with information as well as with stories. Recipe books and cards in the home corner can stimulate reading as the children play at cooking. Occasionally, ask them to draw or write about a cooking activity, perhaps making a group or class book. Describing the process of a cookery activity will help improve children's ability to sequence the order of events. Finally, link stories (see Chapter 10), poems and rhymes with cooking activities.

Technology

There are many links with technology. Children will begin to learn that tools are designed for a particular job and this influences the materials and shape of kitchen equipment. Through discussion, they will eventually develop the ability to choose tools appropriately. Show them how to use equipment safely and encourage an awareness of the safety of others. Although it is too difficult for very young children to design complete recipes, you can sometimes offer them choices when making sandwiches (see page 18) or pizza faces (see page 39) so they begin to make decisions for themselves. At the end of each activity, evaluate how well the recipe went, discuss any difficulties and how these could be overcome next time.

Talk about where goods are sold and how advertising and packaging influence our choices. Ask the children to design their own boxes, wrappings, bags and labels. Similarly, talk about where children eat food (home, school, café, restaurant) and the advantages or disadvantages of each environment. Challenge the children to design their own eating environment in the home corner.

Art

Attractive presentation of food is an important factor in enticing children to eat and is especially helpful in promoting new, healthier options. Making edible pictures of faces on sandwiches or pizzas not only makes cooking fun but may also tempt reluctant eaters. Children need to discuss how colour, shape and texture influence our attitude to food.

Many art activities can involve the use of food. Drawing food from observation is an excellent way of understanding the structure of a cauliflower or the texture of a pineapple. Collage pictures can be made from dried food, for example, pasta, pulses, beans (not red kidney beans which are poisonous until cooked) and seeds. Many fruits and vegetables can be used for printing while play dough (flour, salt and water) is a popular modelling material.

Geography

Food is an important aspect of geography. Buying the ingredients for a cooking activity can involve children in identifying different kinds of work — shopkeepers, farmers and so on.

Discussing the sources of food will help children begin to understand the differences between food from natural resources and processed or manufactured food. Looking at food labels for the country of origin will promote a greater awareness of the world and the need to transport food. Remember to include food in displays about other countries and use multicultural recipes whenever possible (see Chapters 8 and 9).

History

Historical links can be made by investigating the differences between the food available in the past and the present. How many parents ate kiwis when they were a child? Why are they more common today? Some foods have been eaten for several thousands of years. For example, cabbage is an ancient vegetable which was being eaten by the Chinese thousands of years ago. Children are also fascinated by cooking utensils and equipment from the past. If possible, borrow items from parents or museums and compare them with their modern equivalents.

RE

Food is often associated with religious customs and festivals. For example, eggs have played a major role in religious rites and customs. The Christian tradition of giving eggs on Easter Sunday dates back to the pre-Christian Anglo-Saxon festival of Eostre. Find out about different customs and try out significant recipes. Look out for religious stories in which food is an important feature, for example, 'The feeding of the five thousand' (Christian) or the story about Guru Gobind Singh which led to all temples having a kitchen (Sikh).

PE

Opportunities for PE arise through dance miming the growing of food or cooking activities such as stirring, rolling and whisking. Children can also be encouraged to mime the behaviour of food as it is cooked such as the popping of popcorn or the boiling of eggs. Physical co-ordination and fine motor control are improved by many processes involved in food preparation such as mixing, spreading, slicing and kneading.

Music

Don't forget to link cookery activities to music by learning songs about food. Many nursery and finger rhymes refer to food – Little Miss Muffet, Oranges and Lemons, Five Fat Peas and Oats and Beans and Barley Grow. Dried food can also be used to make shakers and children can experiment with producing sounds from *old* kitchen equipment (tin lids, spoons, funnels, graters).

Social education

Finally, many important social skills can be fostered through cooking activities. Children will learn to co-operate with others, share equipment and take turns. Discussions may also include polite behaviour and table manners. For example, do children keep their elbows off the table, wait until everyone is served and ask to leave the table?

Before you start

Chapter one

As with any activity undertaken with early years children, thorough preparation is vital to the success of the project. On the one hand this involves the safe and hygienic preparation of food and equipment to be used while, on the other, a sensitivity to gender issues is required along with an awareness of any restrictions placed on children due to diet, allergies or religious customs.

Safety must be a priority in any cookery activity. Remember to consider the safety aspects of the food itself as well as the more obvious safety aspects of equipment. Similarly, the storage of food and equipment needs to be given careful consideration.

Although current legislation (Food Safety Act 1990 and Food Hygiene Regulations 1991) applies to food being prepared for sale, it contains much sound advice and provides a sensible guide to early years teachers. Local Environmental Health Officers are also a good source of information. The Pre-School Playgroups' Association (PPA) offers helpful advice in their Food and Hygiene in Playgroup Information Sheet and Appendix II in *Good Practice for Sessional Playgroups*. The PPA can be contacted at 61–63 King's Cross Road, London WC1X 9LL.

Special considerations

Gender
Be sensitive to gender issues associated with cookery and try to promote a positive attitude towards these activities. Most boys will be eager to join in with cookery but some may already have developed the attitude that it is only for girls. Don't accidentally reinforce this attitude by always asking 'What does mummy cook?' or 'How does mummy make pastry?' In conversations, remember to refer to fathers or other male members of the family as cooks. It may also be possible to talk about male

chefs who have written recipe books or present cookery programmes on television.

Allergies
Before undertaking any activities with food, it is important to consult parents to discover any potential problems. Some children may be on special diets for health reasons, such as children suffering from diabetes or coeliac disease. Other children may have allergies to particular foods. Common allergies include cow's milk and food additives like colouring agents such as tartrazine while more unusual allergies include wheat, peanuts or certain fruits.

Culture and religion
It is also essential to take any special religious concerns into consideration. Check with parents to discover any dietary customs associated with religious beliefs. Many customs are related to the eating of meat. For example, Jews and Muslims do not eat pork whereas Sikhs and Hindus do not eat beef. Some religions do not believe in eating meat at all. Religious customs are not solely concerned with meat but can also include dairy produce. For example, not all Hindus will eat eggs or cheese. It is also wise to check any fasting periods such as the Jewish Yom Kippur or Muslim Ramadan.

Vegetarians
Some children are vegetarians in that they avoid any food directly or indirectly derived from the slaughter of animals, birds or fish. This can include products such as gelatine, aspic and lard. Vegans also exclude all dairy products and eggs and sometimes honey. Most of the recipes included in this book will be suitable for vegetarians (none contain meat but one or two include fish) but may not be appropriate for vegans.

Hygiene

Establish a regular routine with the children before they start cooking and explain the reasons for each rule. Make sure they put on aprons which are reserved for cooking only. These need to be easy to clean and washed regularly. If necessary, ask the children to roll up their sleeves and tie back any long hair. Ask them to wash their hands and clean their nails thoroughly. If anyone has a cut on their hand, cover it with a plaster and remind the children not to lick their fingers during food preparation. They should also avoid coughing or sneezing over food and rewash their hands after going to the toilet, touching anything dirty and preparing and eating food.

Children need to understand why it is important to keep the cooking area and equipment spotlessly clean. Work surfaces should be cleaned thoroughly and occasionally wiped with mild disinfectant. If classroom tables are being used, they should be covered with a PVC-coated fabric table-cloth. Use disposable cloths for wiping up any spills and tea towels should only be used to dry dishes (not hands) and must be washed regularly. If possible, it is better to allow dishes to drain rather than dry them up. All equipment should be in good condition and any cracked crockery should be replaced because it could harbour germs. Similarly, buy white plastic chopping boards in preference to wooden ones which are more difficult to keep clean.

Equipment safety

Children also need to know and understand the reasons for certain safety rules. Keep a first aid kit available in case of accidents. Show them safety equipment, such as fire extinguishers and fire blankets, oven gloves and heat resistant mats, and talk about their purpose. Make the children aware of the

need to keep all inflammable materials well away from the cooker. Show them how to turn saucepan handles inwards to reduce the likelihood of accidents and explain that a cooker can be extremely hot even if it does not appear to be so. Whenever you use electrical appliances, warn children about the dangers of electricity, such as touching plugs with wet hands and the importance of avoiding trailing flexes. Always wipe up spills on the floor immediately to prevent accidents.

It is vital for all adults supervising cooking activities to agree a clear policy on what is safe for children to do. You need to decide on the amount of responsibility to give to the children. It is important to ensure children are actively involved and not just watching an adult. The whole experience will be meaningless unless they are allowed to do as many of the tasks as possible. On the other hand, however, safety constraints may limit what you think they should do. For example, do you all agree it is too dangerous for children to stir saucepans on a hob or chop ingredients with sharp knives? Write out a safety policy which can easily be handed to any new adult helper. Always teach children the safe use of tools such as how to hold a knife properly.

Food safety

With very young children, it is wise to avoid recipes which include more dangerous processes such as deep fat frying or boiling jam. If a saucepan catches on fire, switch off the cooker and smother the pan with a fire blanket. Never use water.

All eggs should be cooked until both white and yolk are solid, as the government still advises people not to eat raw eggs. Beware of recipes such as mousses which still include this.

Avoid using whole nuts with children under five because choking or inhaling whole nuts can be dangerous. Use peanut butter or chopped or ground nuts instead.

Extra care should be taken with any recipes which involve cooking meat and poultry. Frozen meat must be thawed completely before use and cooked thoroughly at the correct temperature to avoid dangerous bacteria. Keep a separate chopping board and knives for preparing raw meat.

Never leave any food uncovered and keep flies away. Also avoid leaving unsuitable food in warm temperatures for long periods. Always check the 'use by' dates on any ingredients and discard any which are out of date. To avoid any pesticide or insecticide residue, wash fresh produce thoroughly and discard any outer leaves. Peeling will also remove surface residues but it has the disadvantage of reducing the fibre content of the recipe at the same time.

Always pre-heat the oven to the specified temperature so that food is cooked at the correct temperature for the right length of time. This is important to ensure any bacteria are destroyed.

Equipment

Facilities for cooking with early years children vary tremendously. Some are lucky enough to have purpose-built kitchens while others only have a small space in the classroom or another part of the building. Many classes have to overcome the problem of no direct access to hot water. Even if the facilities are poor, however, it is still possible to make simple recipes for drinks, salads and sandwiches which do not require a cooker or expensive equipment.

All equipment needs to be chosen with care. If it is to be shared by many classes, it needs to be portable – cookers on wheels, utensils and tools on racks or in baskets. Centrally stored equipment must be kept in a cupboard separate from other school equipment (especially science) to avoid cross-contamination. Also, all cookery equipment must be used solely for cookery activities.

Take care when siting a cooker, especially in a classroom. Try to position it against a wall away from the door so that a clear escape is available in case of fire. Never site a cooker in a small lobby or narrow corridor. Finally, cookers and other electrical appliances must be regularly maintained.

Don't forget to include timing devices among the cookery equipment – egg/sand timers, alarm clocks, special cookery timers and cardboard clock faces to show the beginning and end of cooking times. Traditional balance type scales are good for reinforcing concepts such as heavier than, lighter than, balances with and so on. Whenever possible, borrow modern electrical appliances such as whisks, blenders, food processors to enable children to compare them with traditional methods.

Food storage

Take care to store food hygienically and at the correct temperature. If cooking is only an occasional activity, use fresh ingredients and transport perishable or frozen foods in a cool-bag. If you are going to store ingredients on the premises over a longer period, make sure they are kept cool, dry, away from direct sunlight and in airtight containers (plastic boxes, jars). If food is transferred from its original packaging, always label the new container clearly, including any important information such as 'use by' dates.

Again, food needs to be kept separately from other school equipment and the 'use by' dates need to be checked regularly. Obviously, if perishable and frozen foods are to be stored for a short period, they need to be kept in a fridge. Make sure the temperature of the fridge is checked regularly to ensure it is cold enough (1–5°C, 34–41°F) and that it is defrosted and cleaned regularly. Cover food stored in the fridge but avoid touching fatty foods with cling film.

Size of group

Occasionally, it may be appropriate to have the whole class cooking at the same time but, on the whole, it is more satisfactory to work in small groups of up to six children. This will reduce the need for lots of equipment and allow the adult to give more attention and help to each child. With this in mind, *all the recipes in this book are designed to serve six*.

Context

Whenever possible, try to provide a real purpose for cookery activities. This could take the form of sharing the food with other people such as parents, another class or elderly people. Alternatively, the focus may be a special event such as a party, religious festival, picnic or outing. Approaching cookery activities in this way will allow the children to be involved in planning menus and choosing food appropriate to the occasion. An extension of this could be to make decorations for the table, design invitations and organise a suitable environment.

Eating the results!

Any cookery activity with early years pupils should be exciting and fun. The educational value is mostly in the activity itself and not solely in the end product. Therefore, it is not essential for every child to eat the final product. If children are forced to eat what has been cooked, then they are going to become anxious about every cookery activity. Try to adopt a relaxed attitude where children are encouraged to taste the food if they want to but reluctant children are allowed to say 'No, thank you'.

Sometimes children will eat something they would not normally try purely because they have helped prepare it and they can see friends and adults enjoying it. Don't despair even if several of the children take one mouthful and decide they don't like what has been cooked. If the children have actively taken part in the process and been tempted to taste something new then it has been a valuable experience. Children can be very conservative in their food preference and will stick rigidly to what is familiar to them — it may very well be a slow process, enticing them to be more open in their attitudes. To avoid a great deal of waste food, make small quantities and put suitable waste food out for the birds.

When choosing a recipe, take into consideration when the children will eat the results. If they are going to eat it on the premises, make sure it is not too near a main meal. If they are going to take it home, think about how they are going to transport it hygenically and without accidents!

The structure of the recipes

Within each chapter, the recipes are ordered according to difficulty so that those recipes with few ingredients and simple processes appear first. For ease of use, each of the recipes is presented in a similar format.

What you need
This section gives a list of the items necessary to make the recipe. For convenience, it has been divided into Ingredients and Equipment. It is assumed that the children will work in small groups of six, so each recipe has been designed to serve six small portions. The quantities given use the metric system of measurement. Whenever possible, involve the children in buying the ingredients. Always gather together all the ingredients and the equipment before you start the activity and wash any fresh produce thoroughly. Once again, allow the children to help in these preparations.

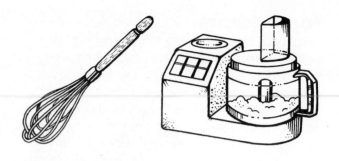

What to do
This section gives simple, step-by-step instructions on how to make the recipe. Allow the children to do as many of the tasks as possible and encourage them to work in pairs if some tasks are more physically demanding. For example, one child can hold the bowl while another uses the whisk or one can hold the grater while the other rubs the carrot up and down on it. If very young children find some of the processes laborious, let them do some of it manually and then finish the process using an electrical appliance such as a food processor. If the oven is to be used, remember to set it to warm up to the correct temperature at the beginning of the activity and warn the children not to touch it.

Discussion
This section shows how to maximise the educational content of the activity by highlighting what to look for and links with other subjects. It gives examples of questions which could be asked but these are not meant to be followed rigidly. You may not have time to use all of them or the children may lead the conversation into other equally educational areas.

Follow-up activities
These are extension activities which develop further cross-curricular links. Sometimes these activities can be undertaken while the food is cooking and on other occasions they will require more time.

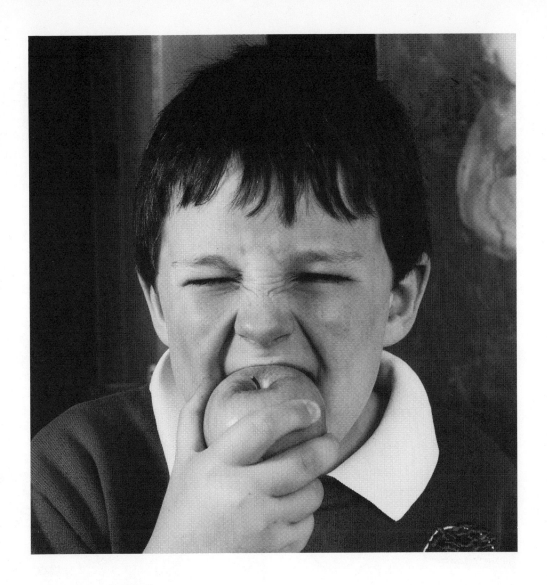

Snacks

Chapter two

Snacks are popular with very young children who, unlike adults, cannot go for long periods in between meals. Unfortunately, many common snacks offered to children, such as crisps and sweets, are not particularly healthy. The following snacks are simple to make and can be used to introduce children to the wide range of healthier alternatives.

Talk with the children about when they eat snacks and what they choose to eat. If the children are allowed to bring snacks for playtime, conduct a survey over one week to record the different types of snack.

It is unrealistic to suggest that children should never eat unhealthy snacks but it is important for them to know which ones to eat in moderation. Discuss the healthier options available to them such as fresh or dried fruit, raw vegetables, soup, wholemeal bread and crackers. Make a group or class picture book in the shape of a smiling face to illustrate these healthy options.

Sandwiches

What you need
Ingredients: 6 slices wholemeal bread, 6 slices white bread, polyunsaturated margarine, small quantities of fillings such as fromage frais, curd cheese, Cheddar cheese, cucumber, cress, tomatoes, onion, radishes, carrots, pineapple chunks, apple.
Equipment: a plate for each ingredient, a grater, 6 knives, 3 spoons, different shaped pastry cutters, 6 small plates.

What to do
Allow the children to help prepare the ingredients by washing and slicing the fruit and vegetables and grating the Cheddar cheese and carrots. Place each ingredient on a separate plate within easy reach of the children.

Invite the children to choose any 2 slices of bread — wholemeal, white or one of each and suggest that they cut their bread into interesting shapes for sandwiches, either with the knife or with the shaped cutters.

Allow the children to choose whether to spread each bread shape with margarine, fromage frais or curd cheese and explain that they can either make open sandwiches or conventional closed ones. They can use any combination of the remaining fillings and should try to make their sandwiches look attractive. Give each child a small plate on which to arrange their sandwiches.

Discussion
Compare and contrast the wholemeal and white bread, focusing on the colour, shape, texture and smell. Which type of bread do the children prefer? Explain that bread is a healthy choice for a snack because it is low in fat and contains carbohydrates, protein, vitamins, minerals and fibre (see chart on page 6). Ask the children to describe the shapes they are making with their bread.

Talk about the fillings the children choose. Do you always need to spread bread with margarine before adding other fillings? Invite the children to alter the shape of the fruit and vegetable fillings by cutting, twisting or bending. Ask them to describe their own choices of filling and compare these with the preferences of others. Sort the children into sets according to who has used fromage frais, cucumber and so on. Talk about why we need to eat a balanced diet to keep fit and healthy, for growth and repair, energy and warmth.

Follow-up
Convert the play house into a sandwich bar. Would it be a 'take away' or more like a restaurant? Make pretend sandwiches and rolls with play dough, Plasticine, clay, thin pieces of sponge or thick card. Involve the children in designing and making signs, posters and packaging to be used in their sandwich bar.

Date and apple spread

What you need
Ingredients: 200g fromage frais, 1 red apple, 12 dates (stoned), 3 sprigs of parsley for garnish, 2 or 3 small wholemeal crackers for each child.
Equipment: a bowl, metal spoon, 6 knives, 6 small plates.

What to do
Tip the fromage frais into the bowl and stir it to an even consistency.

Wash and cut the apple in half and then quarters. Then chop the apple very finely, discarding the core and pips. Stir the chopped apple into the fromage frais. Now chop the dates finely and stir them into the fromage frais mixture. Chop the parsley finely and sprinkle on the top as a garnish.

Give each child a plate, a knife, 2 or 3 crackers and some of the spread to put on to their crackers.

Discussion
Describe the colour and texture of the fromage frais. Explain that it contains little or no fat and so is a very healthy food to eat.

Talk about the colour, shape and texture of the outside of the apple and compare it with the inside. When cutting the apple, use it to demonstrate fractions — halves and quarters. Count how many pips there are. Do the children know that these are the seeds? What other fruits have pips?

Explain the purpose of a garnish. What other types of garnish would be suitable?

Follow-up
Make a variety of different foods (apples, sausages, pizzas, cakes) from coloured play dough or Plasticine. Cut them into halves and quarters and discuss how many pieces they make each time.

Sardine boats

What you need

Ingredients: 75g sardines in sunflower oil, 1 tablespoon lemon juice, 2 tablespoons natural yoghurt, 25g cottage cheese, half a cucumber, 6 lettuce leaves, 6 thin baby carrots.

Equipment: scales, a tin opener, large plate, magnifying glasses, tablespoon, bowl, fork, spoon, sieve, plastic ruler (used only for cooking), 6 knives, 6 small plates, 6 knives and forks.

What to do

Drain off the sunflower oil and place the sardines on a large plate, cut them in half and remove the back bone. Put the sardines into a bowl with the lemon juice and mash them with a fork until smooth.

Sieve the cottage cheese and add it and the yoghurt to the sardines. Beat until smooth.

Give each child a lettuce leaf, a knife and a small plate. Ask them to cut or tear the lettuce into strips and arrange it on the plate so it looks like the sea. Then give each child a piece of cucumber (approximately 6cm long) and ask them to cut it in half lengthways to make two boats (see Figure 1). Arrange the boats on the sea of lettuce and spoon some of the sardine mixture on to the top of each boat. Scrape or peel the baby carrots and cut them into short sections. Push them into the sardine mixture to form funnels.

Discussion

Talk about the appearance of the sardines. Do the children realise they are fish? Which parts of the sardine's body have been removed? Use magnifying glasses to study the back bone. Give each child one of the back bones when it is removed and ask them to gently pull it apart so they can see each little segment.

Compare the texture of the cottage cheese before and after it is sieved. How does the cottage cheese and the yoghurt change the sardine mixture? Compare the height of the carrot funnels and discuss how the children are going to arrange them. Will they put the same size and number of funnels on each boat?

Follow-up

Find out more about bones. Look for pictures of fish, animal and human skeletons in information books and make a collection of real bones. Can the children tell which animal the bone comes from and which part of the body it belongs to? Does the size, shape and weight of the bone relate to its function?

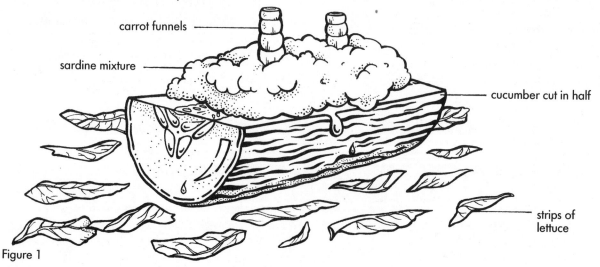

carrot funnels

sardine mixture

cucumber cut in half

strips of lettuce

Figure 1

Humpty Dumpty eggs

What you need
Ingredients: a box of cress, 3 eggs, water, a 5-minute sand timer, quarter of a yellow pepper, 2 tablespoons tomato purée, 1 extra egg for observation purposes.
Equipment: a saucepan, hob, scissors (used for cooking only), colander, bowl, tablespoon, wooden spoon, small coloured plate, 6 knives, 6 small plates, 6 knives and forks.

What to do
Put the 3 eggs into a saucepan, cover with water and boil for 5 minutes until hard boiled. Use the sand timer to time the eggs.

Cut the cress with the scissors, wash thoroughly and drain in a colander. Wash the pepper, remove the seeds and slice into thin strips.

When the eggs are hard boiled, allow them to cool and then shell them. Cut the eggs in half lengthways then carefully remove the yolks and put them into the bowl. Add the tomato purée and stir to make a thick paste.

Give each child a plate and ask them to arrange some cress on it to look like grass. Then give them half an egg white, which is to be Humpty Dumpty's head and body (hollow side down). Invite them to take a small amount of the tomato paste, roll it gently in their fingers and use it to add features to the egg white body. For example, they can add a blob for hair, two small spheres for eyes and roll cylinders for arms, legs and mouths. Alternatively, they may wish to cut the thin slices of yellow pepper to make some of the features. Can they make their Humpty Dumpty look as though he is falling on to the grass? (See Figure 1).

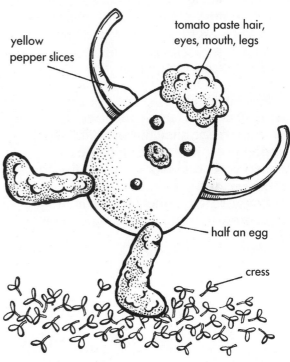

yellow pepper slices

tomato paste hair, eyes, mouth, legs

half an egg

cress

Figure 1

Discussion
Before boiling the eggs, allow the children to hold them gently and encourage them to describe the size, shape, colour, texture and smell. Do they know what the egg looks like inside?

Break the spare egg on to a coloured plate so that the children can see the liquid state of the white and the yolk. Is the white really white? Ask the children to predict what effect boiling will have on the white and the yolk. Compare their predictions with the hard-boiled eggs. How are the eggs different? Emphasise the change of state from liquid to solid.

Look carefully at the cress before cutting it. Identify the roots, stem, leaves and seed cases. How many leaves does each piece of cress have? Which part of the plant do we eat?

As the tomato purée is being mixed into the egg yolk, describe the changes that take place. As the children decorate their Humpty Dumpty shape, talk about the choices they make. Will they use the paste or the yellow pepper to make each feature? Can they suggest alternative ingredients? Is Humpty Dumpty going to have a happy or sad face?

Follow-up

Draw Humpty Dumpty faces on the outside of egg shell halves with felt-tipped pens. Moisten a small pad of cotton wool and place it inside the egg shell. Sprinkle a few cress seeds on to the cotton wool pad and keep them moist as they grow into Humpty Dumpty's hair.

Bubbly toast

What you need

Ingredients: 6 slices wholemeal bread, 130g Cheddar cheese, 4 eggs, 4 teaspoons milk, pepper.
Equipment: scales, magnifying glasses, a metal knife, 2 cheese graters, 2 plates, 2 bowls, a teaspoon, wooden spoon, metal spoon, whisk, one-minute egg timer, baking tray, grill and oven, 6 small plates, 6 knives and forks.

What to do

Cut the cheese into large cubes and ask two children to grate it. One child holds the grater over a plate while the other grates the cheese.

Grill the bread on one side and then sprinkle the grated cheese on the untoasted side. Separate the eggs and beat the egg yolks with the milk and pepper. Whisk the egg whites until they hold their shape and fold into the egg yolks. Spoon the egg mixture on to the cheese.

Place the slices of bread on a baking tray and bake at 180°C/350°F (Gas Mark 4) for 10 to 15 minutes until golden brown. Serve one piece of bubbly toast for each child on a small plate.

Discussion

Look at each of the ingredients in turn and ask the children if they know where it comes from, for example bread comes from wheat, eggs from chickens and so on.

Before toasting, ask the children to feel the bread and look closely at its texture and colour. Magnifying glasses might be a useful aid to observation. Compare the crust with the inside. Show the children the bread as it is grilled. Where does it go brown first? Once the bread is toasted, invite the children to describe the differences between the toasted and untoasted side.

Mark the level of the egg white on the outside of the bowl before and after whisking. Why has the volume increased? Once the toast has been baked, encourage the children to describe how the egg white mixture has changed.

Follow-up

● While the bubbly toast is cooking, experiment with one or two extra slices of bread. Cut one slice of bread very thinly and one thickly and compare the rate of browning under the grill. Allow one slice to burn slightly (not too much in case it ignites). Compare the colour, texture and smell of this slice with untoasted bread.
● Give the children copies of photocopiable page 92 and ask them to match the various foods to their origins. Can the children add one or two examples of their own?

Carrrot and parsnip soup

What you need

Ingredients: 25g polyunsaturated margarine, 500g carrots, 250g parsnips, 1 small onion, 1 vegetable stock cube, 600ml water, a pinch of ground nutmeg, a pinch of black pepper, 300ml semi-skimmed milk.
Equipment: scales, 6 knives, 2 measuring jugs (different shapes), a hob, saucepan, wooden spoon, 5-minute sand timer, kettle, 6 small bowls, 6 spoons, 3 sieves, 3 bowls, a food processor/blender, a blindfold.

What to do

Peel and chop the carrots and parsnips into small pieces. Peel the onion and chop finely. Melt the margarine in the saucepan and fry the vegetables for 5 minutes, stirring occasionally.

Crumble the stock cube into the jug, boil the water in the kettle and pour on to the cube. Stir until dissolved. Add to the vegetables, bring to the boil and simmer for 30 minutes until the vegetables are tender.

Allow the soup to cool then divide it equally between the three bowls. Ask the children to work in pairs, taking turns to hold the bowl and sieve a small amount of soup. If this is too time consuming, use a food processor or blender to purée the soup.

Add the milk, nutmeg and pepper and return the soup to the saucepan to heat it through. Pour the soup into the small bowls and warn the children to be careful in case it is too hot to eat immediately.

Discussion

Describe the colour, shape and texture of each vegetable. Compare the inside of the vegetables with the outside. How are they different? Taste a small amount of each raw vegetable. How does frying change them?

Compare the measuring jugs. Are they made of the same material? Why does it help if the jug is transparent? Test to see if 300ml looks the same in both by pouring 300ml water from one jug into another.

While the soup is cooking, play a smelling game with the children. Allow them to smell a piece of uncooked parsnip, onion and carrot and the nutmeg and pepper with their eyes open. Then blindfold one child at a time and see if they can identify each substance without looking.

Why is sieving a good idea and what other foods are sieved? Compare sieving the soup by hand and mixing it in the food processor.

Follow-up

Make a list of other electrical appliances which are used when cooking and collect some of them together. Draw one from observation and explain its purpose and how to operate it. Discuss the safety rules involved with using electrical appliances.

Salads

Chapter three

The main ingredients of many salads are vegetables and fruit. These are very nutritious because they are low in fat and high in fibre, vitamins and minerals. The bright colours of many salad ingredients make them attractive to children and may inspire art activities. Greater variety and interest can be added by including unusual ingredients, such as exotic fruits, raw cauliflower or broccoli, cold pulses and pasta.

Whenever possible, increase the level of fibre by including the skins of fruit and vegetables. Make sure they are washed thoroughly to remove any traces of pesticide.

The following salad recipes contain a wide variety of salad ingredients and dressings. They are simple to make and can easily be altered or adapted. For example, several of the recipes could be presented in a pitta bread pocket (see 'Coleslaw in a pocket') or made into a picture (see 'Fish-shaped salad') and many of the ingredients changed to suit seasonal availability.

Decorative salad ingredients

One way of adding interest is by cutting salad ingredients into unusual shapes (see Figure 1). Some children may be able to create these shapes on their own but others may need adult assistance. Whenever possible, challenge the children to invent their own interesting shapes. Always slice or cut the salad ingredients into small pieces because many young children are put off by large chunks which are difficult to chew.

Radish flowers:

Wash and trim ends off radish.

Cut slits in top ⅔ down.

Chill in water until petals open.

Carrot flowers:

Wash and peel carrot. Trim off ends.

Cut into short sections.

cuts

Make 'v' shaped cuts along length of carrot sections.

Cut across carrot into slices.

Tomato cups:

Wash tomato and remove stalk.

Cut zigzag shapes around middle.

Pull gently apart.

Celery tassels:

Wash and trim ends off celery stems.

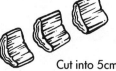

Cut into 5cm sections.

cuts

Cut thin strips ⅔ down celery.

Chill in water until strips curl over.

Spring onion tassels:

Wash and trim ends off spring onion. Remove the white part.

cuts

Cut thin strips ⅔ down spring onion.

Chill in water until strips curl over.

Figure 1

Carrot and watercress salad

What you need

Ingredients: 500g carrots, 50g raisins, 75g watercress, 1 tablespoon sunflower oil, juice of half a lemon.

Equipment: scales, a tablespoon, lemon squeezer, jug, spoon, 3 graters, 6 knives, 6 forks, 6 small plates.

What to do

Peel the carrots and ask the children to work in pairs to grate them (one holding the grater while the other rubs the carrot up and down on the grater).

Chop the watercress finely and give each child a small plate. Ask them to arrange some watercress and grated carrot on the plate in an interesting way. Talk about possible different arrangements (see Figure 1). Older children can use coloured crayons to draw their design on paper first but make sure they do this away from the food preparation area and wash their hands before handling food. Share out the raisins and arrange these on top of the salad.

Squeeze the juice of the lemon into the jug. Add the sunflower oil and stir vigorously until well mixed. Allow the children to spoon their preferred amount of dressing on to their salad.

Discussion

Talk about the benefits of eating salads and discuss the children's preferences for various salad ingredients. As well as providing fibre, carrots are a good source of vitamin A and watercress is rich in iron, calcium and vitamins A and C.

Look closely at the watercress and name the various parts — stem, leaves, roots. Discuss the growing conditions necessary for watercress. What other food plants grow in water (rice)?

Compare the lemon juice and the sunflower oil. Identify any similarities or differences in colour, thickness, smell, feel and taste. What happens when the oil is poured on to the lemon juice and the two liquids are mixed together?

Which salads look most attractive and why? Can the children suggest pairs of other salad ingredients which would make attractive combinations?

Follow-up

Play a memory game based on salads. The first child says 'Into my salad, I will put . . .' and names an appropriate ingredient. Other children then take turns to repeat the previous suggestions and add one of their own so that the list gradually increases.

Different arrangements of salad on plate

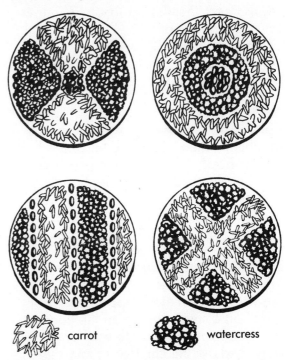

Figure 1

Pink potato salad

What you need

Ingredients: 500g small potatoes suitable for salads (Charlotte, Belle de Fontenay, Maris Peer), 2 small beetroots, 75g low-fat yoghurt, 1 orange.

Equipment: scales, 2 saucepans, a hob, lemon squeezer, 6 knives, 1 large bowl, 6 small bowls, 6 spoons, 6 forks, a glass.

What to do

Boil the potatoes whole with their skins on until cooked. Boil the beetroots whole until cooked. Allow both the potatoes and beetroots to cool before handling.

Share out the potatoes and ask each child to cut them into small pieces and place these in their own small bowl. Rub the skin off the beetroots and chop them into small pieces. Squeeze the juice from the orange into the large bowl then stir in the yoghurt and the chopped beetroots.

Spoon a small amount of the yoghurt and beetroot mixture into each small bowl and ask the children to mix it evenly into their potatoes.

Discussion

Examine the outside of the potatoes and then cut one in half and discuss the differences in appearance. Draw attention to the liquid which appears when the potato is cut. Can the children guess what it is? Taste a small piece of raw potato and describe it. Observe a piece of raw potato regularly over a two-hour period and describe any changes which occur.

Compare the colour of the water before and after cooking the beetroot. How has it changed? What effect will the beetroot have on the yoghurt? Does the colour of food make it more or less attractive to eat? Would the children eat blue bananas or green custard?

Follow-up

Talk about the various forms in which we eat potatoes — mashed, boiled, baked, roast, chipped and so on. Conduct a survey to find out each child's favourite and record the data in the form of a chart (use a computer if appropriate).

Coleslaw in a pocket

What you need
Ingredients: 6 mini wholemeal pitta breads, 125g red cabbage, half an apple, 50g sultanas, 1 stick of celery, 3 tablespoons fromage frais, 1 tablespoon lemon juice, 1 teaspoon honey, a pinch of cayenne pepper.
Equipment: scales, a bread knife, tablespoon, teaspoon, jug, 6 spoons, 6 knives, 6 plates for serving, 6 small bowls.

What to do
Slice the red cabbage, apple and celery very finely. Give each child a bowl and place a small amount of each ingredient in each bowl. Share out the sultanas among the six bowls.

Make the dressing in the jug by mixing together the fromage frais, lemon juice, honey and cayenne pepper. Invite the children to spoon some of the dressing over their salad (if desired) and toss it so that all the ingredients are covered by a little dressing.

Slice open one side of the pitta breads (an adult will probably need to do this) and give one to each child together with a small plate. Allow the children to spoon their coleslaw into the pitta bread pocket.

Discussion
Look at each of the coleslaw ingredients and identify whether it is a fruit (the part of the plant holding the seeds) or a vegetable. Explain that some things that we think of as vegetables, such as courgettes and tomatoes, are really fruits. Which part of the plant do we eat with celery and cabbage?

Count the number of sultanas and ask the children to predict how many each child will get when they are shared out. Share them out and then discuss whose estimate was closest.

Ask the children to describe each ingredient used in the dressing. Can they identify each one just by smell? Where does honey come from? Do the other ingredients come from a plant or animal?

Talk about the use of a 'pinch' for measuring small quantities. Compare an adult pinch with a child's pinch. Link this with any previous measuring experiences with handspans or footsteps.

Follow-up
Compare the prices for each ingredient. Which is the most/least expensive? Ask the children to put three or four of the ingredients in order according to price. Use real or cardboard coins to show the correct money for each ingredient.

Rice salad

What you need

Ingredients: 75g brown rice, 2 spring onions, 50g tinned sweetcorn, 50g frozen peas, 1 tablespoon sunflower oil, 1 tablespoon soy sauce, 1 tablespoon lemon juice, ½ teaspoon ground ginger, 12 crispy lettuce leaves.
Equipment: scales, a tin opener, tablespoon, teaspoon, hob, sieve, jug (½l), spoon, glass, large bowl, 2 saucepans, 6 knives, 6 forks, 6 plates.

What to do

Bring 2 jugfuls of water to the boil in one of the saucepans, add the rice and cook until tender. Bring 1 jugful of water to the boil in the other saucepan, add the peas and cook until tender.

When the rice is cooked, use the sieve to separate the rice from the water and then measure the water in the jug. Place the rice in the bowl. Use the sieve to drain the cooked peas and then measure the water in the jug. Place the peas in the bowl. Finely chop the spring onions and add to the rice together with the sweetcorn.

Put the sunflower oil, soy sauce, lemon juice and ground ginger into the empty jug and stir together until well mixed to make the dressing.

Give each child a plate and one or two lettuce leaves. Ask them to cut the lettuce leaves finely and place them around the edge of their plate. Spoon the rice mixture into the middle and allow the children to add the required amount of dressing to the rice.

Discussion

Look closely at the uncooked rice and describe its colour, shape, size, texture and taste. Put a few grains of rice into a glass of cold water to see if it will soften.

Compare and contrast the tinned sweetcorn with the frozen peas. What are the similarities and differences? Name other tinned and frozen foods. Why do we store food in tins or in a freezer?

When the rice and peas have been cooked, measure the remaining water and compare with the original amount. Where has the water gone? Look for condensation in the room. Compare the cooked rice and peas with their uncooked state and describe any changes. Count the number of spoonfuls of rice mixture given to each child. Do they all want the same number or do some want more or less?

Follow-up

Look at each of the ingredients and talk about the type of shop where they could be bought. Discuss the variety of food shops (greengrocer's, grocer's, baker's, fishmonger's, farm shops) as well as supermarkets. Make books for each shop to show what goods can be bought there.

Salad patterns

What you need
Ingredients: 200g beansprouts, 2 button mushrooms, half a red pepper, 1 cucumber, 1 tablespoon sunflower oil, 3 tablespoons vinegar, mint leaves.
Equipment: scales, a tablespoon, jug, 6 knives, 6 spoons, 6 small plates, a container for each of the beansprouts, mushrooms and pepper.

What to do
Slice the button mushrooms thinly. Remove the seeds from the pepper and slice thinly. Place the beansprouts, mushrooms and pepper in separate containers.

Cut the cucumber into six 4cm pieces and give one piece to each child. Give each child a small plate and a knife then ask them to use the salad ingredients to make patterns on their plate (see Figure 1). Invite them to change the shape or size of each ingredient by cutting. For example, they could slice the piece of cucumber into circles (which could be cut into halves or quarters), dice it into small cubes or chop it into oblongs. Remind them to make sure their pattern repeats correctly throughout (one piece pepper, four beansprouts and so on).

Put the sunflower oil and vinegar into the jug. Chop up the mint leaves finely and stir into the oil and vinegar mixture. Allow the children to spoon the required amount of dressing over their salad.

Discussion
Look carefully at the beansprouts and describe their appearance. Is it possible to see any of the mung beans from which the sprouts are growing? Name other dishes which include beansprouts (widely used in Oriental and Indian cooking).

Talk about the shapes created when the ingredients are cut in different ways. Compare the sizes of the ingredients and discuss how these can be altered by cutting. Create two or three patterns with the ingredients and ask the children to predict what comes next in the sequence. Compare the finished patterns on the plates and identify several of the sequences. Which plate is most attractive and why?

Watch closely when the oil and vinegar are placed in the jug. Describe what happens. Does the oil always float on top of the vinegar? Which is heavier, the oil or the vinegar?

Follow-up
Make repeating patterns with vegetable prints. Dip pieces of vegetable (potato, carrot, onion, Brussels sprouts) into paint and press gently on to a piece of paper. Make repeating patterns with different colours and shapes.

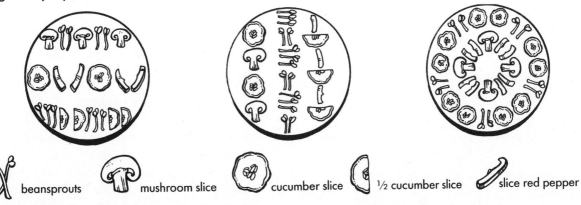

beansprouts   mushroom slice   cucumber slice   ½ cucumber slice   slice red pepper

Figure 1

Fish-shaped salad

What you need
Ingredients: 100g wholewheat pasta spirals, 1 courgette, 3 tomatoes, 213g tin red kidney beans, 2 tablespoons tomato puree, 2 tablespoons vinegar, 1 tablespoon sunflower oil, 150ml water, 1 teaspoon dried basil.
Equipment: scales, a tin opener, tablespoon, jug, teaspoon, saucepan, hob, colander, small plate or dish for the courgette, tomatoes and kidney beans, 6 knives, 6 small plates, 6 knives and forks for serving.

What to do
Boil some water in the saucepan, add the pasta spirals and cook for 10 minutes until tender. Drain in the colander and allow to cool.

Cut the ends off the courgette, slice it thinly and place on a dish or plate. Slice the tomatoes thinly and put on the dish or plate. Open the tin of red kidney beans, drain off the liquid and empty on to the dish or plate.

Invite the children to use the pasta, courgette, tomatoes and red kidney beans to make a picture of a fish on a small plate of their own (Figure 1). They can use any combination of these ingredients to design their own fish.

Make a salad dressing by mixing the tomato purée, vinegar, sunflower oil and basil with 150ml water. Serve the salad dressing separately in the jug with a spoon so that the children can control how much they want to spoon over their fish picture.

Discussion
Describe the pasta before and after cooking. Look for changes in the colour, size, shape and texture of the pasta.

How can we tell when the water is boiling? Take the opportunity to warn the children about the dangers of boiling water. Which ingredients will be eaten raw and which will be cooked? Discuss the benefits of eating raw fruit and vegetables (cooking can reduce the vitamin content of some vegetables and fruits). Remind the children that the red kidney beans have been cooked and that they should never be eaten raw because they are poisonous. Talk about the reasons for cooking food. For example, the heat kills germs (meat), some foods taste nicer (potato) and cooking can soften tough tissue to make it more digestible (popcorn).

As the children design their fish, talk with them about the shapes and colours of the ingredients chosen. Compare the fish designs and discuss which are the most attractive and why.

Talk about the salad dressing. What is a dressing and why do we use it?

Follow-up
Invite the children to design a salad of their own. Ask them to draw and label the ingredients they would use (they could write on a large salad bowl shape or make a picture with their ingredients) and describe any dressing they would choose.

½ slice tomato   pasta spiral   kidney bean

courgette slice   ½ courgette slice

Figure 1

Hot savoury food

Chapter four

The recipes in this chapter show how a diverse range of savoury foods can be presented to young children. Many of the recipes can be altered to include different ingredients according to preference or seasonal availability.

Although many children opt for sweet foods, savoury foods can be just as appetising and a great deal healthier. Many savoury recipes are based on nutritious ingredients such as vegetables, pulses, rice and pasta but, unfortunately, it is easy to inadvertently change these healthy ingredients into an unhealthy recipe. Avoid recipes which include large quantities of fat (cream, butter) or which use high fat methods of cooking (deep fat frying). Similarly, do not overcook vegetables as they may lose many of their vitamins.

Make savoury recipes more appealing by encouraging children to choose their own combination of ingredients (see Baked potato surprises) or design their own decoration (see Carrot quiche and Pizza faces).

If food is cooked and served on the premises at lunchtime, look at the menu and identify the savoury foods. Conduct a survey to find out the most popular savoury dish from those served in one week. Record the results and invite one of the cooks to talk about (and if possible demonstrate) how it is made.

Stuffed tomatoes

What you need
Ingredients: 3 large beef tomatoes, 15g polyunsaturated margarine, 1 small onion, 50g wholemeal bread, 1 tablespoon horseradish sauce, parsley.
Equipment: scales, a tablespoon, saucepan, hob, bowl, wooden spoon, baking sheet, oven, 3 graters, 6 spoons, 6 knives, 6 small plates, 6 forks.

What to do
Cut the tomatoes in half. Give each child half a tomato, a spoon, a knife and a plate. Ask them to scoop out the tomato flesh with the spoon and put it on to their plate. Then chop the flesh into small pieces and tip it into the bowl.

Chop the onion finely and fry gently in the margarine. Add the cooked onion to the bowl and stir into the tomatoes.

Ask the children to work in pairs to grate the bread (taking turns to hold the grater or rub the bread on it). Stir the breadcrumbs into the tomatoes with the horseradish sauce. Save some of the parsley for garnish and chop some finely to add to the tomato mixture.

Fill the tomato shells with the mixture, place them on to a baking sheet and bake in the oven at 200°C/400°F (Gas Mark 6) for 20 minutes. Allow to cool, then place one on each plate and garnish with sprigs of parsley.

Discussion
Compare the outside of the tomatoes with the inside, identifying the various parts (stalk, skin, flesh, juice, seeds) and describing the structure. Talk about the number of halves in one tomato, two tomatoes and so on.

As the children grate the breadcrumbs, talk about the graters. Are they all the same size and colour? Are they all made of the same materials? Why are some holes large and some small? Grate the bread on the different sized holes and compare the resulting crumbs.

Look at the label on the horseradish sauce to find the ingredients. Explain that horseradish is a plant and allow the children to taste a small amount. Encourage them to describe the taste and name any other 'hot' tasting foods.

Follow-up

Draw half a tomato from observation. Use oil pastels on a pale green sugar paper and encourage the children to fill the paper with their picture. Suggest they overlap and blend the colours by smudging with a finger to create new colours.

Baked potato surprises

What you need

Ingredients: 3 potatoes, 6 tablespoons fromage frais, a selection of filling ingredients to mix with the potato (for example mushrooms, spring onions, pickle, chutney, tinned sweetcorn, grated cheese, chopped parsley).
Equipment: an oven, knife, tablespoon, tin opener, grater, a dish or plate for each ingredient, spoons, 3 metal skewers, 6 small bowls, 6 small spoons, 6 potato mashers or forks, a baking sheet, 6 plates, knives and forks for serving.

What to do

Bake the potatoes in the oven at 200°C/ 400°F (Gas Mark 6) for 1 hour. This time can be reduced if each potato has a skewer pushed through the middle before baking. Obviously, access to a microwave would reduce the time still further.

Encourage the children to help prepare the ingredients for the filling by grating the cheese and chopping the parsley, mushrooms and spring onions. Put each ingredient on to a plate or dish with a spoon.

When the potatoes are cooked, cut them in half and allow them to cool down enough to be handled. Give each child half a baked potato and ask them to use a small spoon to remove the flesh from the skin, putting the potato flesh into a small bowl of their own. Put one tablespoon of fromage frais into each bowl and use a fork or potato masher to cream the potato.

Invite the children to choose any combination of the filling ingredients to mix into their creamed potatoes. Spoon the final mixture back into the potato skins, place on a baking sheet and cook in the oven at 200°C/400°F (Gas Mark 6) for 10 minutes until the filling is golden brown.

Discussion

Talk about the reason for putting a skewer in each potato. Have an extra potato without a skewer for comparison. Have the children ever seen skewers being used in other recipes?

Look closely at the potatoes and describe their colour, shape, texture and size. Count the number of eyes and discuss their function.

When the baked potatoes are cut in half, watch the steam rise from the inside. How has cooking changed the inside and outside of the potato? Compare mashing the potato with a fork and a potato masher. Which is easier and why?

Talk with the children as they choose their filling ingredients. How does chutney or pickle change the colour of the potato? Which combination of flavours do they think will go together well?

Follow-up
Use potatoes for simple weighing activities. Ask the children to find three things heavier than one potato, three things lighter and three things the same weight. Challenge them to record and then compare their findings. Why are some of the results different? For example, one potato might be the same weight as three bricks while another might be as heavy as six bricks.

Baked bean parcels

What you need
Ingredients: 12 slices wholemeal bread, polyunsaturated margarine for spreading, a tin of baked beans (low in sugar and salt), 50g Cheddar cheese.
Equipment: scales, a tin opener, grater, tablespoon, bun tin, large round pastry cutter, oven, 6 knives, 6 small plates, 6 knives and forks for serving.

What to do
Give each child 2 slices of bread and ask them to use the pastry cutter to cut out a circle from each slice of bread.

Spread margarine on one side of both of the circles. Place one circle margarine side down into the bun tin and press it into the shape. Put one or two tablespoons of baked beans on top of each circle of bread. Press the other circle of bread margarine side up on top of the baked beans.

Grate the cheese and sprinkle a little on each baked bean parcel. Cook in the oven for 5 minutes at 200°C/400°F (Gas Mark 6).

Discussion

Look carefully at the tin opener and ask the children to explain how it works. If it has cogs or wheels, can the children describe their function? Talk about the safety aspects of using a tin opener.

Describe the appearance, smell, taste and feel of the baked beans. What would the children normally eat with baked beans? Can they name other types of bean? Which ones do they buy in tins?

Compare the appearance of the parcels before and after cooking. How have the parcels changed in colour and texture? What has happened to the cheese?

Follow-up

Use any left over pieces of bread to make a bird cake. Chop it into small pieces and mix it with other ingredients such as dried fruit, nuts, seeds, mashed potato, grated cheese and so on. Weigh all the dry ingredients together then divide their weight in half. Add this weight of melted fat. Chill in the fridge and then place on a bird table. Record which birds visit the bird table to eat the bird cake.

Spaghetti with lentil sauce

What you need

Ingredients: 1 small onion, half a red pepper, 2 tablespoons sunflower oil, 1 teaspoon basil, 397g tinned tomatoes, 100g red lentils, 1 tablespoon tomato purée, 400ml water, 300g wholewheat spaghetti.

Equipment: scales, a tablespoon, teaspoon, jug, tin opener, 6 knives, 6 chopping boards or plates, 2 saucepans, a hob, sieve, 6 knives, forks and plates for serving.

What to do

Chop the onion and pepper into small pieces. Put the oil into a saucepan and fry the onion and pepper for 5 minutes. Then add the basil, tomatoes, lentils, purée and water. Bring to the boil and then simmer uncovered for 20 minutes.

Half fill the second saucepan with water and bring to the boil. Add the spaghetti and boil rapidly, uncovered, for 10 to 15 minutes. Drain the spaghetti in the sieve and serve with the sauce.

Discussion

Compare the size, shape and colour of the two saucepans. Discuss which materials have been used in their design. Why wouldn't a metal handle be suitable on a saucepan? Look to see if either of the saucepans has a non-stick surface on the inside and discuss the reasons for this.

Ask the children to describe the shape and size of the tin of tomatoes. What are tins made out of? They are usually iron plated with tin. Which part of the tin should we avoid touching once it is opened?

Describe the colour, shape, texture, smell and taste of the uncooked spaghetti. Show the children the spaghetti at intervals during cooking so that they can observe the changes in colour and pliability. Compare the cooked spaghetti with the uncooked and describe any similarities or differences.

Follow-up

Investigate food and drink tins and cans. Make a collection for sorting and comparing (size, shape, manufacturer, contents, ring pull or not). Be careful with sharp edges on used tins — cover them with plastic caps to make handling safer. Scratch a tin and a can, leave them outside for a week and then compare. Do the children notice any changes? Test to find which tins and cans have iron in them by finding out which are attracted to magnets.

Carrot quiche

What you need

Ingredients: 150g polyunsaturated margarine, 200g white self-raising flour, 200g potatoes, 100g carrot, 2 eggs, 150ml semi-skimmed milk, 1 teaspoon chives, ground black pepper.
Equipment: scales, a jug, teaspoon, bowl, hob, knife, potato peeler, potato masher, grater, tablespoon, 5-minute sand timer, 2 wooden spoons, 2 saucepans, 6 small glass fluted flan dishes, an oven, 6 knives and forks for serving.

What to do

Peel the potatoes and cut them into small pieces. Place in a saucepan, cover with water and cook until soft.

Put 100g of the margarine into a bowl and beat until soft. Add the flour and mix well. Drain and mash the cooked potatoes and stir into the flour mixture. Knead on a floured surface and cut into 6 pieces.

Give each child a piece of dough and ask them to pinch off a small piece to make a number. Roll the small piece into a thin cylinder and then shape it into any number from 0 to 9. Then give each child a small flan dish and ask them to press the remaining dough evenly into the shape of the dish.

Grate the carrot coarsely. Melt the margarine in a saucepan and cook the carrot gently for about 5 minutes. Remove from the heat and allow to cool.

Beat the eggs into the milk in the jug. Chop the chives and stir into the milk with the black pepper and the cooked carrot. Use the tablespoon to put some of the mixture into each flan case then place the dough number gently on top.

Cook in the oven at 190°C/375°F (Gas Mark 5) for 20 to 30 minutes until the filling is set and golden brown.

Discussion
Compare the potatoes before and after cooking. What are the similarities and differences?

Look closely at the flour and describe its appearance, smell, texture and taste. Where does flour come from? Talk about the feel of the dough and encourage the children to think of as many words as possible to describe it. Suggest each child makes a different number so they can identify their own flan.

Use a sand timer to time the cooking of the carrots. How does cooking change the carrots? Watch carefully as each ingredient is added to the milk and describe any changes that take place. Do they float or sink?

Look for changes in the quiche after cooking. How is the colour and texture different? Ask each child to identify their number and, when the quiches are cool enough to handle, use these to reinforce any current mathematical concepts.

Follow-up
● Find out more about flour. Make a collection of samples of different sorts of flour (white, wholemeal, wheatmeal and so on) and compare them. Do the children realise flour originates from a plant? If possible, have examples of wheat plants so the children can see the seeds which are processed into flour.
● Collect plant and processed samples of other cereals such as oats and barley. Arrange for a visit to a farm to see cereal crops growing.

Pizza faces

What you need
Ingredients: 225g white self-raising flour, 1 teaspoon baking powder, 25g polyunsaturated margarine and a little extra to grease the baking sheets, 50g Cheddar cheese, 150ml semi-skimmed milk, 397g tinned tomatoes, 1 small onion, half a green pepper, half a yellow pepper, 1 tomato, 2 slices Cheddar cheese.
Equipment: scales, a teaspoon, jug, bowl, sieve, grater, rolling pin, 2 bowls, 6 knives, a tin opener, blender, spoon, greaseproof paper, 2 baking sheets, oven, 6 plates, 6 forks.

What to do
Sieve the flour and baking powder into the bowl. Rub in the margarine until it resembles fine breadcrumbs. Grate the 50g of cheese and stir into the flour. Add the milk and mix into a dough. Knead on a floured surface until smooth. Cut the dough into 6 pieces and allow each child to roll out their piece of dough into a circle.

Drain off the juice from the tinned tomatoes, place the tomatoes into the blender and purée them. Allow each child to spoon the tomato purée over her pizza until it is completely covered.

Slice the onion, green and yellow pepper and tomato into rings. Invite the children to use any combination of these ingredients together with the slices of cheese to make faces on their pizza.

Grease the baking sheets using the greaseproof paper and place 3 pizzas on each. Bake in the oven at 180°C/350°F (Gas Mark 4) for 20 minutes.

Discussion

Talk about the reasons for adding milk to the dry ingredients. What does 'knead' mean and why do it? Name other occasions where kneading is necessary. Discuss the importance of using a floured surface.

Suggest the children predict and then count how many spoonfuls of tomato purée are needed to cover their pizza face. Which pizza face needed most/least?

When decorating their face, encourage the children to cut the vegetable rings into different shapes as well as using them whole. Talk about the features which they want to include on their face (eyes, nose, mouth, ears, hair, eyebrows, beard and so on) and encourage them to make each design different (see Figure 1).

When they are cooked, describe how heat has changed the ingredients. Compare the designs of the pizza faces.

Follow-up

Write group or individual stories about a pizza. An adult could act as scribe for very young children while they draw the illustrations. Suggest they start by describing the pizza — 'I am a pizza. I have two tomatoes for eyes . . .' and then think of an interesting adventure for it. Was it the biggest or smallest pizza in the world? Where was it made? Did someone eat it or did it have a more unusual ending?

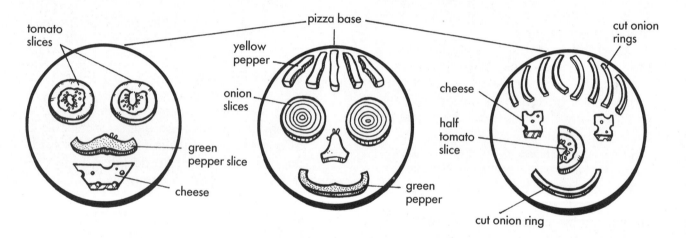

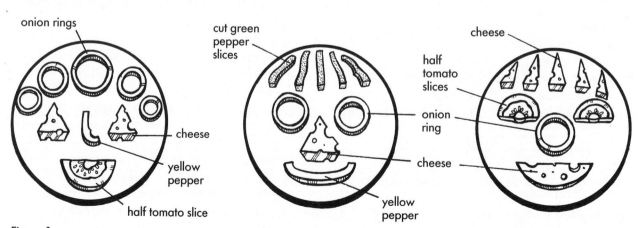

Figure 1

Puddings

Chapter five

Puddings are always a firm favourite with children and involving the children in their preparation can lead to a greater awareness of which foods are good for us and why we should not eat too much of certain foods. The following recipes include hot and cold dishes and show how a wide range of fruits can form the basis of many puddings. In most cases, seasonal substitutes can be made to the ingredients.

Puddings are a favourite with most children but many desserts contain large proportions of sugar, fat and refined white starches. Try to find recipes with low sugar and fat contents. Use fresh fruit and resist the temptation to add sugar to it. Introduce the children to exotic fruits (kiwi, star fruit and mango) when they are in season by occasionally adding one to a fruit salad or as decoration to a cold dessert.

If a recipe requires tinned fruit, always choose fruit canned in natural juices and not syrup. Often puddings which include cream can be made healthier by substituting fromage frais or natural yoghurt. Commercially produced jellies often have a high sugar content and artificial colourings. Try making jellies with fruit and gelatine (or agar-agar for vegetarians) as in the Apricot jelly recipe. Discuss the healthier alternatives to puddings such as dried or fresh fruit, yoghurt or fromage frais.

Fruit salad

What you need
Ingredients: 1 banana, 1 apple, 2 oranges, 1 kiwi, 18 grapes.
Equipment: 6 small chopping boards (or plastic plates), 6 serrated knives, 6 small fruit dishes (or clean yoghurt pots), a lemon squeezer, sharp knife (for adult use only), 6 small spoons.

What to do
Give each child a chopping board, knife and fruit dish. Wash the apple and grapes thoroughly in case they have been sprayed with fungicide or pesticide.

Chop the banana in half and give the pieces to two children to slice thinly. Ask the two children to share their slices among all 6 fruit dishes.

Cut the apple in half and then into quarters. Remove the core and give four of the children a quarter of the apple to slice. Ask each child to share their slices among all 6 fruit dishes.

Cut both oranges in half. Put aside one half and give the others to three of the children. Ask them to peel off the skin, remove any pips and divide the orange into segments. If the oranges are large, cut each segment in half. Ask each child to share their segments among all 6 fruit dishes.

Peel the kiwi (an adult may need to do this) and cut it in half. Give it to two children to slice and ask them to share their slices among the 6 fruit dishes.

Give each child 3 grapes and ask them to cut them in half and remove any pips. Add the grapes to their fruit dish.

Ask two children to squeeze the juice from the remaining orange half. One child can hold the lemon squeezer while the other presses the orange on to it. Pour a little juice over each dish of fruit and toss the fruit with a spoon.

Discussion
Before making the fruit salad, look closely at each fruit in turn. What colour, shape and texture is it? Describe the smell of each fruit. Hold each fruit gently and say which feels hard or soft. Can the children close their eyes and identify each fruit purely by touch? Look to see where each fruit was attached to its plant.

Why is it important to wash fruit thoroughly before eating? When each fruit is sliced, draw the children's attention to the inside. Is it a different colour? Are there any pips and how are they arranged? (In some fruits the seeds are less obvious. For example, on bananas the seeds are usually only small dark dots arranged in rows along the length of the banana because cultivated bananas have been bred to cut down the size of the seeds.) Point out that the seeds are often protected by a tough skin (peel) on the outside and a soft protective tissue (flesh) on the inside.

Follow-up
• Keep the fruit pips and ask the children to bring others from home to make a collection. Use them for mathematical activities such as sorting, ordering according to size and counting. Plant the pips and see if any of them germinate.
• Give the children the photocopiable resource sheet on page 93. Cut out the pictures of fruit and stick them on to another piece of paper in pairs, matching the inside with the outside.

Hot orange cups

What you need
Ingredients: 3 oranges, 25g raisins, 300ml water, 25g ready-to-eat prunes, 1 teaspoon cinnamon.
Equipment: scales, a jug, teaspoon, 6 knives, 1 grapefruit knife, 6 chopping boards or plates, a saucepan, hob, 6 small plates for serving, 6 spoons.

What to do
Cut the oranges in half and remove the flesh with the grapefruit knife (an adult will need to do this). Give each child the flesh from half an orange and ask them to take out the pith and chop the flesh finely. Put the flesh and any juice into the saucepan.

Chop the prunes into small pieces and add these with the raisins to the saucepan. Pour in the water and add the cinnamon. Poach gently with the lid on for 5 minutes.

Allow the mixture to cool slightly. Give each child half an orange shell on a small plate and ask them to fill their shell with the mixture.

Discussion
Compare the grapefruit knife with the other knives, discussing the similarities and differences. Why does the grapefruit knife have a curved shape and serrated edge? How does the design of each knife aid its function? Talk about the safe handling of knives (always holding the handle, carrying and storing them with the sharp blade pointing downwards, never playing with them).

When the oranges are cut in half, examine them carefully and name the various parts — peel, pith, pips, flesh. Discuss why some foods are dried and ask the children to name other dried fruit.

Smell the cinnamon and see if it floats or sinks on the water. If possible, have some cinnamon sticks to compare with the ground powder. Explain that the sticks come from the bark of a tree in the laurel family. Warn the children about not touching their eyes after handling spices because some may cause irritation.

Follow-up
Dried fruit makes a healthy substitute for sweets. It is high in fibre and although it contains sugar (fructose), is less harmful to teeth. Introduce the children to a range of dried fruit by holding a tasting session. Try sultanas, raisins, currants, dates, figs, apricots, pears, apples, prunes. Which do the children prefer and why? Experiment by soaking a piece of each fruit in hot water. How have they changed after two hours or if left overnight?

Pineapple sorbet

What you need
Ingredients: 432g crushed pineapple in natural juice, 50g castor sugar, 1 tablespoon lemon juice, 300g natural yoghurt.
Equipment: scales, a tin opener, tablespoon, bowl, saucepan, hob, wooden spoon, sieve, shallow plastic container with lid, freezer, freezer thermometer, 6 small dishes, 6 spoons.

What to do
Separate the pineapple and the juice by draining it in the sieve. Pour the juice into a saucepan and put the pineapple into a bowl. Add the sugar and the lemon juice to the saucepan and heat until the sugar has dissolved. Leave it to cool.

Stir the yoghurt into the pineapple and then stir in the cooled juice. Pour this mixture into the plastic container, put on the lid and freeze until solid. Take the sorbet out of the freezer at least an hour before serving so that it softens slightly. Serve in the small dishes.

Discussion
Smell the pineapple and ask the children if it reminds them of something. Can any of the children describe a pineapple? Look on the label of the tin to see if there is a picture. What other foods can be bought in tins? Why are some foods tinned?

How does the yoghurt change the pineapple? Look carefully at the sorbet before it is put in the freezer so that the children can compare it with the frozen sorbet. Use the freezer thermometer to compare the temperature of the sorbet before freezing, when half frozen and when completely frozen.

Feel the outside of the dishes before and after the sorbet has been put into them. Describe any changes. Invite the children to describe how the sorbet melts in the dish as they eat it and help them realise there has been a cycle from liquid to solid to liquid.

Follow-up
Discuss the reasons for freezing foods. Find out about other types of preserved food – salted, pickled, bottled, tinned, dried and so on. Make a set of foods for each category, using pictures from magazines or empty packets, bottles or tins (use plastic caps to cover the rough edges on the top of used tins). Talk about the need to store food correctly to avoid it going bad and help the children to recognise when food is unsafe to eat by smelling and looking for signs of decay.

Apricot jelly

What you need
Ingredients: 250g ready-to-eat dried apricots, the juice of half a lemon, 15g gelatine, water.
Equipment: scales, a lemon squeezer, jug, saucepan, hob, food processor or blender, kettle, spoon, jelly mould, plate, 6 small dishes, 6 spoons.

What to do
Put the apricots in the saucepan with 300ml water. Simmer for 20 minutes until the apricots are tender.

Boil 300ml water in the kettle and pour it into the jug. Sprinkle on the gelatine and stir until dissolved.

Place the cooled apricots and their juice into the food processor (or blender) and purée. Add the gelatine mixture and process again. Stir in 150ml cold water and pour the jelly into the mould. Chill in a fridge until set.

Dip the outside of the mould into hot water to loosen the jelly and turn out on to a plate. Serve in the small dishes.

Discussion
Ask the children to describe how they would normally make a jelly. Explain that shop bought jellies usually contain sugar and artificial colours but it is possible to make a jelly without these. Explain that the gelatine is going to make the jelly set. Encourage the children to describe the gelatine granules when dry and when added to the hot water. Does the gelatine float or sink? What happens to it and how does it change the water? Compare the characteristics of the jelly before and after chilling. After tasting the jelly, contrast it with shop bought jellies.

Look carefully at the dried apricots and describe their colour, shape, texture and smell. If possible, compare with an ordinary apricot. Predict how the dried apricots will change when cooked.

Explain how to use kettles safely. For example, plugs should not be touched with wet hands, the lead should not trail where it can accidentally get caught on something and hands should not be placed near the spout when hot steam is coming out.

Follow-up
Set up some simple experiments to find other substances which dissolve in water. Try sugar, flour, salt, vegetable oil, cornflakes and dried peas. Older pupils could also investigate if the results differ according to the water's temperature.

Rhubarb crunch

What you need
Ingredients: 500g rhubarb, fresh orange juice, 150g natural yoghurt, 4 digestive biscuits, a pinch of mixed spices.
Equipment: scales, a saucepan, plastic bag, rolling pin, hob, spoon, sieve, bowl, food processor, 6 serving dishes, 6 knives, 6 spoons.

What to do
Give each child 1 or 2 sticks of rhubarb and ask them to chop it into small chunks. Put the rhubarb into the saucepan with a little orange juice. Gently cook the rhubarb until it is soft and then leave to cool.

Try sieving the cooled fruit first and then finish making it into a purée in the food processor. Stir in the yoghurt and spoon into the serving dishes.

Crush the biscuits with the spices in a plastic bag (sealed with a tie) by rolling over them with a rolling pin. Sprinkle the crumbs on top.

Discussion
Discuss which part of the plant the rhubarb comes from (stem) and remind the children never to eat the leaves which are poisonous. Compare the sticks of rhubarb to reinforce measuring vocabulary such as longest, shortest, as long as, longer than and so on.

Watch the steam rising from the rhubarb as it cooks and look for condensation under the saucepan lid. Do the children know what the steam and condensation are?

Ask the children to describe how cooking has changed the colour, shape and texture of the rhubarb. Discuss the meaning of the word 'purée' and how easy or difficult it is to sieve the fruit. Contrast this with using the food processor. Discuss how the fruit purée is altered further when the yoghurt is added. As the children eat the dessert, contrast the characteristics of the soft puréed fruit mixture with the crunchy topping.

Follow-up

Ask one or two of the pupils to draw and colour a giant picture of a dish of rhubarb crunch. Think of as many words as possible to describe the fruit (soft, creamy, thick) and the topping (hard, crunchy, sweet). Write the words on labels and stick them on to the appropriate place on the picture.

Lemon pudding

What you need

Ingredients: a lemon, 50g polyunsaturated margarine and a little extra for greasing the dish, 50g castor sugar, 2 eggs, 50g white self-raising flour, 150ml water.
Equipment: scales, a lemon squeezer, jug, wooden spoon, 2 bowls, 2 whisks, a spoon, greaseproof paper, an ovenproof dish, oven, 6 small dishes, 6 spoons.

What to do

Cream the margarine and the sugar until light and fluffy. Separate the eggs and stir in the yolks. Mix in the flour. Add the juice from the lemon and then stir in the water. Whisk until smooth.

Whisk the egg white and fold into the mixture. Grease the ovenproof dish and pour in the mixture. Bake in the oven at 180°C/350°F (Gas Mark 4) for 20 to 30 minutes. Serve in the small dishes.

Discussion

Discuss the meaning of the term 'cream' in cookery. Can the children name other recipes where 'creaming' has been necessary? Describe how the 'creamed' mixture changes with the addition of each ingredient.

Cut the lemon in half, name the various parts and talk about its structure. Taste a little of the lemon juice and describe it. What other sour foods can the children name? Discuss the three other categories for taste (sweet, bitter, salty) and ask the children to name examples for each category.

Talk about the reasons for whisking the ingredients. Look carefully at the size and shape of the bubbles.

Discuss the importance of using an 'ovenproof' dish. When serving the pudding, encourage the children to notice how the sponge and sauce have separated into two layers.

Follow-up

Collect labels from lemons to discover their country of origin. Find the country or countries on a map or globe. Discuss why lemons cannot be grown outside in this country and compare our climate with the climate of the country of origin. Encourage the children to use information books to find out how lemons are grown, harvested and transported here.

Cakes and biscuits

Chapter six

Cakes and biscuits will be familiar to all children and, in contrast to many foods the children can make, do not have to be eaten immediately. They form a central part of festivals and celebrations from all cultures and the children's enthusiasm can be channelled into their cooking and related topic work.

Baking cakes and biscuits is a popular activity with early years children but remember to keep a balance between sweet and savoury recipes. Whenever possible, increase the fibre level in recipes by using wholemeal flour, oats and All-bran. Similarly, polyunsaturated margarine can easily be used instead of butter. Leave out any added salt and select recipes with less sugar and fat. Try to avoid adding too many sugary decorations or cream fillings. Instead, substitute dried or fresh fruit and flavoured fromage frais as in the recipe for Sponge cakes.

Talk about the special occasions when cakes are the focus of attention as in birthdays, weddings, Christmas or other religious celebrations. Ask the children to describe their own experiences and bring in any photographs of cakes associated with a special occasion in their family.

The following recipes provide a balance between sweet and savoury cakes and biscuits. Many of the ingredients can be adjusted to create different flavours. For example, the satsumas in the Sponge cake recipe could be substituted by a wide range of alternatives such as pineapples or peaches.

Herb scones

What you need

Ingredients: 125g white self-raising flour, 2 teaspoons baking powder, 25g polyunsaturated margarine and a little extra for greasing the baking tin and spreading on the finished scones, 50g Cheddar cheese, 1 dessertspoon dried mixed herbs, 70ml milk plus a little extra for the top of the scones.

Equipment: scales, an oven, teaspoon, dessertspoon, jug, sieve, bowl, grater, wooden spoon, rolling pin, circle-shaped pastry cutter, pastry brush (used only for cooking), greaseproof paper, baking tray, 6 small plates for serving.

What to do

Sift the flour and baking powder into the bowl and rub in the margarine. Grate the cheese and stir into the mixture. Add the dried mixed herbs and milk and mix to a soft dough.

Knead for a few minutes and then roll out on a lightly floured surface until approximately 3cm thick. Cut into circles with the pastry cutter. Lightly grease the baking tin and place the scones on the tin. Brush the top of the scones with a little milk and bake in the oven at 230°C/ 450°F (Gas Mark 8) for 10 minutes. Cut each scone in half and spread a little margarine on each half (see Follow-up) before serving.

Discussion

Discuss the function of the baking powder, explaining that it makes cakes and biscuits rise by creating bubbles. Demonstrate this by mixing a little flour with water to form a thin cream. Add some baking powder and look for bubbles. Explain that when the baking powder gets hot, even more bubbles (of carbon dioxide) are formed and these make cakes or biscuits rise and lighter in texture. Self-raising flour already has some baking powder in it but more is needed because the methods used in this recipe do not incorporate much air into the mixture.

Do the children know what dried mixed herbs are? Ask them to look carefully at the herbs and describe what they can see. Look at the ingredients label to find out which particular herbs are in the mixture (usually sage, thyme, marjoram, oregano and parsley). If possible, compare them with fresh herbs.

Discuss the purpose of kneading the dough. Can the children name any other recipes which involve kneading? What effect will the milk have on the top of the scones? Leave one scone without any milk for comparison. Ask the children to describe the scones in detail before and after cooking.

Follow-up

While the scones are cooking, make some butter to go with them. Pour the cream from 2 or 3 pints of gold top milk into a small transparent plastic container with a lid. Screw the lid on tightly and shake the milk until the butter is formed (this can take 20 minutes or more). Use a one minute sand timer to time each child's turn at shaking the milk. When the butter has formed, tip off the buttermilk (which the children can taste) and spread on to the scones.

Sesame snail biscuits

What you need

Ingredients: 175g wholemeal self-raising flour and a little extra for the baking sheets, 125g polyunsaturated margarine, 1 teaspoon curry paste, 1 egg, sesame seeds, a little water.
Equipment: scales, a teaspoon, spoon, whisk, pastry brush, 2 bowls, 2 baking sheets, 6 knives, an oven, small plates for serving, a till receipt for the above ingredients plus other till receipts for comparison.

What to do

Put the flour into a bowl and rub in the margarine until it resembles fine breadcrumbs. Separate the egg and add the yolk to the mixture. Stir in the curry paste and mix into a firm dough, adding a little water if necessary.

Knead the dough on a floured surface and then divide it into 6 pieces. Give each child a piece and show them how to make a snail shape (see Figure 1). Invite the children to make snail shaped biscuits with their piece of dough.

Lightly whisk the egg white and brush across the top of each snail. Sprinkle each snail with sesame seeds and press them lightly into the dough. Place the snails on the baking sheets and bake in the oven at 180°C/350°F (Gas Mark 4) for 15 minutes. Serve the biscuits on the small plates.

Roll a small piece of dough into a cylinder.

Roll one end into a spiral shape.

Leave some of the cylinder for the body.

Figure 1

Discussion

Smell the curry paste and look on the label for a list of ingredients. Do any of the children know any of the spices? Explain that spices are the dried aromatic parts of plants such as the seeds, pods, roots, stems or bark. Often, the spices have been ground into a powdered form. Warn the children not to touch their eyes after handling any spices because some spices may cause irritation.

As the children make their snail shapes, talk about spirals. Can they name other spiral shaped foods, for example a Swiss roll? Ask them to describe the egg white on the biscuits. How does it change the surface of the biscuit? Look carefully at the sesame seeds and describe their shape, size, colour and texture. What other seeds do we eat?

Discuss the characteristics of the cooked biscuits. How have they changed? Describe their smell and taste? Suggest other minibeast shapes which could have been made.

Follow-up

● Choose four or five different savoury biscuits (plain, cheese, Marmite, for example) and encourage the children to taste them. Ask them to choose their favourite type of biscuit and record their preferences using sets or pictorial graphs (use a computer if possible). Which biscuit is the most or least popular? How many more children prefer curry flavoured biscuits to plain ones?
● Link with an investigation into minibeasts such as snails.

Tomato puffs

What you need

Ingredients: 40g polyunsaturated margarine and a little extra for greasing the bun tin, 150ml water, 50g white self-raising flour, 2 eggs, 250g cottage cheese, 1 tablespoon parsley, 2 tablespoons tomato purée.
Equipment: scales, a jug, tablespoon, saucepan, hob, wooden spoon, sieve, bun tin, greaseproof paper, spoon, oven, wire rack, knife, 2 bowls, 6 plates.

What to do

Sieve the flour. Put the margarine and the water into the saucepan and heat gently until the fat has melted. Bring the liquid to the boil and remove from the heat. Beat in the flour quickly and return to a low heat, continuing to beat until the mixture leaves the sides of the pan. Allow to cool slightly.

Beat the eggs together in the jug and then beat them, a little at a time, into the flour mixture. Grease the bun tin and spoon some of the mixture into each hollow. Bake in the oven at 220°C/425°F (Gas Mark 7) for 10 minutes and then reduce the heat to 180°C/350°F (Gas Mark 4) for 15 minutes more. Cool on a wire rack.

Sieve the cottage cheese into a bowl and stir in the tomato purée. Chop the parsley finely and add to the cottage cheese. Cut the puffs in half and spoon in the filling. Serve the puffs on the small plates.

Discussion

At regular intervals, show the children the margarine as it melts with the water and ask them to describe what happens. Does the margarine float or sink on the water? What other substance melt? How can we tell when the liquid is boiling?

Watch to see how the mixture changes with the addition of the flour and the eggs. Count the number of spoonfuls placed in each hollow in the bun tin. Describe the cooked puffs in detail. How has the colour, shape, size and texture changed after cooking?

What effect does sieving have on the cottage cheese? Describe the changes caused by adding the tomato purée. Smell and taste a little of the parsley. Which part of the plant are we eating? Can the children predict how many tomato puffs they will each get? Share them to find out.

Follow-up

Use information books to find out about cheese and make a display to convey the information in an interesting way. How is cheese made? What is cottage cheese? How many other different types of cheese can the children find? Collect labels and packging from various cheeses to add to the display.

Apple and pear cakes

What you need

Ingredients: 75g All-bran, 75g ready-to-eat dried pear, 25g brown sugar, 50g apple, 300ml milk, 1 teaspoon vanilla essence, 75g wholemeal flour, 1 teaspoon baking powder, 1 teaspoon ground ginger, margarine for greasing the tin.
Equipment: scales, a jug, teaspoon, grater, wooden spoon, sieve, 2 bowls, greaseproof paper, a bun tin, oven, wire rack, plate for serving, 5-minute sand timer.

What to do

Pour the milk and vanilla essence into the bowl. Add the All-bran, pears and sugar. Leave to soak for 10 minutes.

Sieve the flour and add the baking powder and ground ginger. Stir the dry ingredients into the All-bran mixture. Grate the apple and stir it into the mixture.

Grease the bun tin with a little margarine on some greaseproof paper and put some of the mixture into each hollow. Bake in the oven at 180°C/350°F (Gas Mark 4) for 25 minutes. Cool on a wire rack and then arrange on the plate for serving.

Discussion

Talk about when All-bran is normally eaten. Name other breakfast cereals. How many children eat breakfast cereals? Encourage the children to look carefully at the All-bran in its dry state, describing the colour, shape, texture and taste. Look to see whether the All-bran floats or sinks when added to the milk. How does soaking change the All-bran sugar and pears?

Smell the vanilla essence. Why do we only need a small quantity? If possible, have one or two other essences (lemon, peppermint) available for the children to smell.

Look at the bun tin and count the number of hollows altogether. Then count the number of hollows in each row and column. Use the bun tin as a grid and ask the children to point to specific hollows. For example, the hollow which is 3 across and 2 up, 4 across and 1 up, and so on.

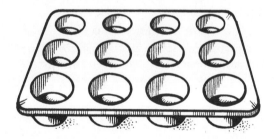

Follow-up

Compare and contrast a collection of breakfast cereal packets. What information is on the packaging? Challenge the children to design the outside of a cereal packet. First of all, unfold cereal packets and reassemble them inside out (adult assistance will be needed for young children). Suggest the children work directly on to the grey card of the packet or else work on paper which can then be stuck on to the box.

Banana cake

What you need

Ingredients: 50g polyunsaturated margarine and a little extra for greasing the tin, 50g castor sugar, 1 egg, 50g wholemeal self-raising flour, 1 teaspoon baking powder, 1 banana, 25g chopped nuts.
Equipment: scales, an oven, teaspoon, wooden spoon, 2 bowls (made from different materials, for example glass and plastic), greaseproof paper, an 18cm sandwich tin, wire rack, plate for serving.

What to do

Cream the margarine and sugar together in a bowl until fluffy. Beat in the egg and then gradually fold in the flour and baking powder. Mash the banana and stir into the cake mixture.

Grease the sandwich tin lightly, pour in the cake mixture and spread it evenly. Sprinkle the nuts on the top and bake in the oven at 190°C/375°F (Gas Mark 5) for 15 minutes. Cool on a wire rack and serve on the plate.

Discussion

Before cooking, compare and contrast the two bowls. Are they the same size, shape, colour and material?

Ask the children to describe the changes as each ingredient is added. Focus their attention particularly on the way in which 'solid' ingredients such as the margarine and banana can change in consistency through certain actions — beating with sugar, mashing.

Discuss the nutritional advantages of eating nuts (a good source of unsaturated fat, protein, vitamins and fibre). Do the children eat nuts in other foods, for example breakfast cereals or peanut butter? Explain that salted nuts are less healthy than unsalted ones. Warn the children of the danger of choking or inhaling whole nuts.

Discuss the reason for allowing the cake to cool on a wire rack. Look for steam or condensation coming from under the cake. How can the cake be cut into six equal pieces? Experiment by folding or drawing on a circle-shaped piece of paper the same size as the cake.

Follow-up

Make a zig-zag book to illustrate the recipe. Invite each child to draw, colour and write about one of the stages in the recipe on a piece of paper. Mount each picture on to coloured sugar paper and sequence them in the correct order. Stick the pictures together to make a zig-zag book which can be displayed for other children to read.

Sponge cakes

What you need

Ingredients: 3 eggs, 50g castor sugar, 75g white self-raising flour, a small amount of polyunsaturated margarine to grease the tin, 100g fromage frais, 1 teaspoon orange marmalade, tinned (in natural juice) or fresh satsumas.

Equipment: scales, a teaspoon, whisk, 1 minute sand timer, 2 bowls, 2 metal spoons, a sieve, Swiss roll tin, oven, greaseproof paper, 6 knives, 6 small plates, large chopping board, pastry cutters (different shapes and sizes — see Figure 1).

What to do

Put the eggs and sugar into the bowl and whisk them together until they become thick and creamy. Allow each child to have a turn using the whisk for 1 minute with a sand timer.

Sieve the flour and fold it into the egg mixture. Grease the Swiss roll tin lightly with margarine and pour the sponge mixture into it. Spread it out evenly and bake in the oven at 200°C/400°F (Gas Mark 6) for 5 to 10 minutes until golden.

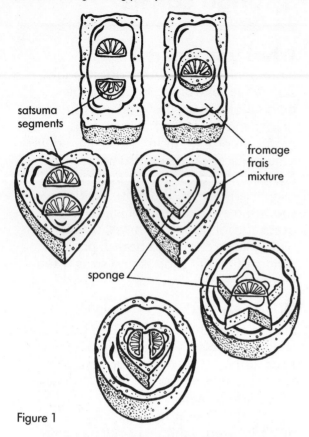

Different designs using pastry cutters.

satsuma segments

fromage frais mixture

sponge

Figure 1

Put the fromage frais into the second bowl and stir in the orange marmalade. Give each child a knife and a plate and ask them to chop some of the satsuma segments finely (reserve some for decoration). Stir these into the fromage frais mixture.

Cover the chopping board with greaseproof paper and tip out the cooked sponge on to it. Allow the sponge to cool. Demonstrate how to make a small sponge cake by cutting out one or two sponge shapes with the pastry cutters, spreading them with a little of the fromage frais mixture and adding satsuma segments for decoration. Explain to the children that they can design their own sponge cakes using any combination of sponge shapes. They can use a single or double layer of sponge. More mature children could also cut out their own square, oblong and triangle

shapes as well as using the cutters. As there will probably be enough sponge for them to make 2 or 3 cakes, encourage them to make each design different (see Figure 1). To avoid waste, suggest they start cutting out their sponge shapes from the edge and place the pastry cutter close to the last shape each time. Ask them to arrange their finished sponge cakes on their small plate.

Discussion

Look closely at the whisk and ask the children to explain how it works. Encourage them to describe what happens as the eggs and sugar are whisked.

Look at the satsumas in detail. Describe their colour, shape, texture and smell. Do satsumas grow in this country?

As the children make their sponge cakes, talk with them about their choice of shapes. Are they going to put a heart shape on top of a circle shape? How many satsuma segments will they use for decoration? Can they suggest another fruit which would have been suitable for this recipe? Discuss the finished cakes and count how many different variations have been designed.

Follow-up

Reinforce mathematical concepts about space and shape. If only one cutter was allowed, how many shapes could you cut from the sponge? Make card templates of each cutter and give the children pieces of paper the same size as the Swiss roll tin. Ask them to choose a shape and estimate how many would fit on to the paper. They can then draw round the shape as many times as possible, covering the paper. Count the number of shapes and compare the total with their estimate. Are there any shapes which tessellate (fit together without leaving any spaces)? Which shapes leave most or least space in between?

54

Drinks

Chapter seven

Drinks are an excellent way of introducing basic cookery skills such as chopping and stirring. They often require simple equipment and no cooking so they are ideal for early years settings with few cookery facilities.

In order to stay healthy, we need to drink plenty of fluids each day. Water makes up about four-fifths of our body weight and is an important aid to digestion. Talk with the children about why we need to drink to replace water lost through urine, sweating and breathing out. How do our bodies tell us that we need more water and why do we get particularly thirsty in hot weather? Contrast the access we have to pure water with people in other countries who have little or contaminated water.

Home-made drinks can be designed to avoid the high sugar content and artificial colours and flavours of commercially-produced drinks. Fresh, unsweetened fruit juice can form a healthy basis for many drinks. Milk-based drinks are also a good choice because milk is a valuable source of calcium and protein. To reduce the fat content in milk, use semi-skimmed for children over two years of age.

Make drinks more exciting by adding different decorative toppings such as fruit, grated nutmeg, coconut and chopped nuts. You could add to the fun by offering straws or making unusual ice cubes (see Floral ice cubes).

The following recipes show how making drinks can develop many skills across the whole curriculum. They are simple to make and many of the flavourings could be altered to create new drinks.

Blackcurrant frais

What you need
Ingredients: 250g fromage frais, 1 litre unsweetened blackcurrant juice, desiccated coconut for decoration.
Equipment: scales, a jug, bowl, whisk, 6 glasses.

What to do
Put the fromage frais into the bowl and pour on the blackcurrant juice. Whisk until well mixed. Pour back into the jug and chill. Serve in the glasses with a little desiccated coconut sprinkled on top.

Discussion
As the fromage frais is tipped from the dish on the scales, encourage the children to notice how the fromage frais

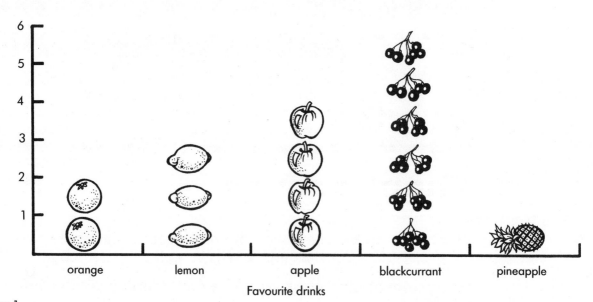

Figure 1

clings to the sides. Compare this to the blackcurrant juice as it is poured from the jug. Which clings most? Describe the colour, texture, smell and taste of the fromage frais. Does it remind the children of another milk product such as yoghurt? Describe how the blackcurrant juice changes the fromage frais.

While waiting for the drink to chill, wash up the equipment and use it for water experiments on capacity. Challenge the children to predict how many glasses full of water will fill the dish on the scales, the bowl and the jug. Record the estimates and then test to find out how many are required.

Predict and describe the effects of sprinkling the desiccated coconut on the drink.

Follow-up
● Conduct a survey to find out the children's favourite flavour of juice. Limit the choice to four or five popular drinks (orange, lemon, apple, blackcurrant, pineapple) and record their preferences using pictures on a graph. Each child can draw and colour a glass full of their favourite juice and stick it in the appropriate column on the graph (see Figure 1). Use the graph to find out which drink is most/least popular and to compare one flavour with another.
● Show the children a real coconut and a picture of a coconut palm tree. Find out more about coconuts.

Banana milk shake

What you need
Ingredients: 300g natural yoghurt, 1 lime, 2 bananas, 600ml semi-skimmed milk, ground nutmeg.
Equipment: scales, a knife, bowl, spoon, fork, jug, lemon squeezer, whisk, 6 glasses.

What to do
Use the fork to mash the bananas in the bowl. Stir in the yoghurt and the milk. Squeeze the juice from the lime and add to the milkshake. Whisk all the ingredients until frothy.

Pour the milkshake back into the jug to make it easier to serve. Pour into the glasses and sprinkle each one with a pinch of nutmeg.

Discussion
Talk with the children about the benefits of drinking milk. Discuss the meaning of the phrase 'dairy products' and see if the children can identify the other dairy product in this recipe. What other products are made from milk?

Describe the changes in the bananas as they are mashed. Cut the lime in half and describe its appearance. Does the lime remind the children of any other fruits? Introduce the phrase 'citrus fruits' to describe oranges, grapefruits, lemons and limes.

How does whisking change the milkshake? Are the bubbles only on the surface or all the way through the milkshake? Suggest other ways of getting bubbles into the liquid.

If possible, provide a whole nutmeg to compare with the ground nutmeg. Smell them both and describe the appearance of each. Look on the label to find the country of origin (nutmegs come from large evergreen trees native to the tropics). Which part of the plant is the nutmeg? (Seed.) Does the nutmeg float or sink on the milkshake?

Follow-up

Make a display to show the variety of products made from milk. Use white paper to cut out the shape of a giant bottle of milk. Then collect labels, wrappers or pictures from magazines of dairy produce to stick on to the giant bottle shape. How many different products did the children find?

Striped cocktail

What you need

Ingredients: 300ml unsweetened blackcurrant squash, 600ml lemonade, 300ml semi-skimmed milk, 6 tablespoons chocolate ice cream.
Equipment: 3 measuring jugs, 6 glasses (tall and thin), a tablespoon, 6 large metal spoons, 6 straws.

What to do

Pour 50ml blackcurrant squash into each glass. Slowly pour 100ml lemonade over the back of the metal spoon into each glass. Suggest the children work in pairs — one holding the metal spoon so it touches the level of the liquid and the other pouring gently. Repeat this process with 50ml milk in each glass. Put 1 tablespoon of ice cream into each glass and add a straw (see Figure 1).

Discussion

Look for sugar on the ingredients list of the three drinks. (Remember that sugar is often present under other names such as glucose or saccharin.) Talk about the disadvantages of drinks with high sugar contents.

Describe the separate layers which appear in the cocktail (the lemonade will become coloured by the blackcurrant squash). Why does the milk stay at the top? Watch the chocolate ice cream as it melts and describe what happens. Try moving the ice cream by blowing gently through the straw. Can you see the liquid passing up the straw? Which layer will the children drink first?

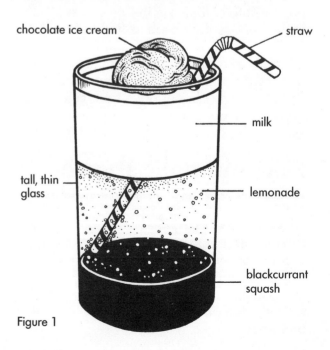

Figure 1

Follow-up

Experiment to see how easy it is to see straws in a variety of liquids. Try: water, blackcurrant squash, milk, washing-up liquid and so on. Also look through the side of the glasses where the straws break the surface of the liquids. Is there any distortion causing the straws to appear to bend? Compare with a straw in an empty glass.

Hot chocolate

What you need

Ingredients: 1 litre semi-skimmed milk, 4 heaped tablespoons drinking chocolate, 6 marshmallows.
Equipment: a saucepan, wooden spoon, tablespoon, measuring jug, bowl, whisk, hob, 6 cups, 6 straws, 6 small spoons.

Discussion

Watch what happens to the milk as it is heated. What rises from the surface of the milk? What appears on the surface of the milk as it gets hotter? How can you tell when the milk is nearly boiled? (It starts to rise up in the saucepan.)

When the drinking chocolate is sprinkled on to the milk, does it float or sink? How does it affect the colour of the milk? What does whisking do to the drinking chocolate?

Feel the outside of the cups before and after the drink has been poured into it. Describe the change in temperature. Do the marshmallows float or sink in the drink? After a few minutes, use a spoon to take them out and look closely underneath. How has the marshmallow changed?

What to do

Bring the milk just to the boil (*an adult must do this*). Avoid full boiling as this results in a skin on the milk which some children dislike. Pour the milk into a bowl and stir in the drinking chocolate. Whisk the milk and drinking chocolate. Make sure the mixture is cool enough before the children start to whisk.

Pour into the cups and put a marshmallow into each one. Give each child a straw and a small spoon.

Follow-up

Look at several examples of decorated party straws and challenge the children to design their own. Use the photocopiable sheet on page 94 for them to record their initial ideas. Once they have tried out their design, they can describe (orally or in writing) the process of making their straws and any difficulties they encountered. Test out the designs on a glass of water and evaluate how well they worked.

Yellow fruit punch

What you need

Ingredients: 300ml water, fresh mint leaves, 1 lemon, 2 grapefruits, 500ml unsweetened pineapple juice, a star fruit.
Equipment: a jug, tablespoon, kettle, wooden spoon, funnel, filter paper, bowl, lemon squeezer, small ladle, 6 knives, 6 glasses.

What to do

Chop the mint leaves finely and add 2 tablespoonfuls to the jug. Boil the water and pour over the mint. Leave to stand for 10 minutes, stirring occasionally with the wooden spoon.

Cut the grapefruits and lemon in half. Cut one slice from each fruit for decoration. Squeeze the juice from the fruits and place in a bowl. Put the filter paper in the funnel and stand it in the bowl then pour the mint and water through it. Add the pineapple juice and stir together.

Cut the fruit slices into halves, quarters or segments. Slice the star fruit. Put the pieces of fruit into the punch and chill in a fridge. (For a hot fruit punch for cold weather, heat the punch gently before adding the fruit.) Ladle the punch and the pieces of fruit into the glasses.

Discussion

Compare the tablespoon, wooden spoon and ladle, describing any similarities or differences. Discuss how the material from which they are made and their overall design aid their function. For example, why is a wooden spoon more appropriate when stirring hot liquids?

How does the shape of the ladle make it easier to serve liquids? Compare several different types of spoon (baby's spoon, metal or china spoon, teaspoon).

Talk about the reason for leaving the mint leaves to stand in the hot water and see if the children can name other substances which are left to infuse (tea, ground coffee).

Compare the halves of grapefruit and lemon, identifying any differences or similarities. Can the children identify the halves purely by smell? All the fruits in this recipe are yellow. What other yellow fruits are there? Name a set of red fruits for a red fruit punch.

Measure the level of the fruit punch before and after adding the pieces of fruit. Why does it change? Does the fruit float or sink?

Follow-up

Investigate funnels and filters. Test the funnel to see which substances pass through easily. Try water, currants, dried butter beans, lentils, crisps and so on. Record the findings. Then experiment to find which liquids or liquids with solids are separated by filtering. Try: gravy, tea made with loose tea leaves, ground coffee and so on. Record the findings.

Raisin fizz

What you need

Ingredients: 2 oranges, 250ml unsweetened apple juice, 600ml sparkling mineral water, 18 raisins.
Equipment: a lemon squeezer, knife, spoon, 2 jugs, 6 glasses, 6 straws.

What to do

Cut the oranges in half, remove the pips and squeeze out the juice. Put the apple juice into a jug with the orange juice. Measure the sparkling mineral water into the other jug and add to the juice. Place the jug in the fridge and leave to chill.

Serve in the glasses with a straw. Give each child two or three raisins to add to their drink.

Discussion

Listen as the bottle of sparkling mineral water is opened and describe any sounds. When the mineral water has been poured into the jug, watch the bubbles. Which direction are they moving and what happens to them? Explain that the bubbles come from a gas called carbon dioxide which dissolves in the water. Can the children suggest other ways of putting bubbles into drinks? For example, shaking, whisking or blowing with a straw.

What happens to the raisins when they are added to the drink? (If the colour of the drink makes it difficult to see, try using plain sparkling mineral water.) Compare with ordinary tap water.

Follow-up

Challenge the children to design a magical drink. Suggest they draw and label a list of ingredients. These can be as fantastic and unusual as the children like. Invite them to describe what happens when anyone drinks this potion. Do they change colour, grow a tail or shrink? Warn the children against drinking any liquid not approved by an adult.

Ice cubes

What you need
Ingredients: water, flavourings (orange, apple, blackcurrant juice), leaves from herbs (various mints, lemon balm, thyme), flowers from herbs (borage, thyme), edible berries (blackberries, raspberries, blackcurrants, redcurrants).
Equipment: ice cube trays (various sizes and shapes), a jug, freezer, 6 knives.

What to do
Coloured ice cubes
Pour juice of different flavours and colours into ice cube trays and freeze overnight.
Leaf cubes
Chop the leaves from herbs finely and place in the ice cube trays. Cover with water and freeze overnight. If the leaves tend to float to the surface, ensure they are suspended in the middle by adding half the water, freezing, topping up with water and then freezing again.
Flower cubes
Place individual flowers from herbs in separate compartments in the ice cube tray, cover with water and freeze overnight.
Berry cubes
Put one berry in each compartment in the ice cube tray, cover with water and freeze.

Release all of the above ice cubes from the tray by running under warm water. Use with any cold drinks.

Discussion
Talk about the ice cube trays. What material are they made of? Count the number of compartments and discuss how they are organised in rows. Are the hollows in the tray cube-shaped or another shape? Challenge the children to find other more unusual shaped containers (different shaped yoghurt pots, balloons) to make ice cubes which are not the normal cube or cuboid shape.

Describe the ingredients used. What colour, shape, texture, smell and taste do they have? Can the children predict how they will change when frozen? Compare their ideas with the frozen ice cubes. Talk about the dangers of poisonous plants and berries.

Study the ice cubes. What happens if you hold one in your hand? Do ice cubes float or sink in the drink? What happens if you push an ice cube down to the bottom of the glass with a spoon and then release it? Measure the level of a drink before and after adding three or four ice cubes.

Follow-up
Time how long it takes for ice cubes to melt under different conditions. Try placing one in a drink, one on a plate, one in a fridge and one in hot water. Challenge the children to predict and record the order of melting and offer explanations for this.

Food for celebrations

Chapter eight

Food is an integral part of many festivals and can provide an insight into the many celebrations of various cultures and faith communities. Often, the same themes appear in festivals all over the world. For example, marking the beginning of a new year, giving thanks for harvests, celebrating the birth of important people and Spring festivals which focus on the planting of crops and the idea of 'new life'.

It is important to check the precise date of many religious festivals because they may vary from year to year. A good source is the Shap Calendar of Religious Festivals (available from The National Society's RE Centre, 23 Kensington Square, London W8 5HN). Also, although many religious festivals have particular foods associated with them, these may vary slightly depending upon the country in which they are celebrated. For example, Muslims in India may eat different celebration foods from Muslims in the Middle East.

Use the festivals celebrated by the children in your early years setting to inspire cookery activities. Whenever possible, invite adults (parents, grandparents, members of religious communities) to talk with the children about celebration food and ask them to demonstrate or lead cookery sessions.

The following recipes are all for foods which are associated with particular celebrations.

Boiled yams

Festival: Ghana Yam Festival, August or September.

What you need
Ingredients: 2 or 3 yams, a little semi-skimmed milk, one small potato.
Equipment: 3 potato peelers, 6 knives, a saucepan, hob, sieve, bowl, potato masher, 6 small plates for serving, 6 knives and forks.

What to do
Peel the yams with the potato peelers. An adult may need to help very young children. Cut the yams into small pieces and place into a saucepan full of water. Boil the yams until tender.

Remove the yams from the hob and allow to cool slightly. Drain off the water with the sieve and place the cooked yams into the bowl. Mash until smooth, adding a little milk if necessary. Serve the mashed yams on the small plates.

Discussion
In West Africa, yams are a staple crop and their harvest at the end of the rainy season is a special time for celebration. Yams from the new crop are offered to the God of the Yam and to ancestors at family shrines. Help the children understand the word 'staple' and name other staple foods (bread, rice, potatoes).

Examine the yams carefully. Use the potato as a comparison and play 'Spot the difference' by asking each child to point out one difference between the yam and the potato. Draw their attention to differences in size, shape, colour, texture, smell and weight.

Try tasting a small piece of raw yam and listing as many words as possible to describe it. As the children take turns to mash the yams, ask them to describe how they have changed after cooking. Do the yams taste the same as potatoes?

Follow-up

Dancing in praise of the Yam God is an important feature of the festival. Suggest the children work in groups to create a dance to honour a staple food such as yam, bread, rice or potato. Encourage them to add percussion sounds to their dance. Each group can perform their dance to the others.

Apple compote

Festival: Rosh Hashanah – Jewish New Year, mid- to late-September.

What you need

Ingredients: 900g cooking apples, the juice from half a lemon, 4 tablespoons honey, 4 tablespoons fresh orange juice, a pinch of nutmeg.
Equipment: scales, a lemon squeezer, tablespoon, ovenproof dish, bowl, wooden spoon, oven, 6 knives, 6 small bowls, 6 spoons.

What to do

Peel the apples and remove the cores. Cut each apple into 6 pieces and place in the ovenproof dish. Squeeze the lemon and pour the juice into the bowl. Add the honey, orange juice and nutmeg and stir together.

Pour the mixture over the apples and bake uncovered in the oven at 160°C/ 325°F (Gas Mark 3) for 30 minutes. Occasionally, baste the apples. When cooked, serve the apples in the small bowls and warn the children to allow the fruit to cool before eating.

Discussion

At Rosh Hashanah, Jewish people have a special meal after visiting the synagogue. During the meal, pieces of apple are dipped into honey to symbolise 'a good sweet year'.

Look at the peeled skin of the apple and contrast one side with the other. Leave one piece of apple on the work surface and record any changes in colour during the cookery session.

Compare the taste of the lemon juice and the orange juice. Introduce the words 'sweet' and 'sour'. Explain that the taste buds on the tongue are organised into areas which detect different tastes — sweet taste buds are at the front while sour taste buds are at the sides. Test these areas with small amounts of lemon and orange juice.

Explain the meaning of the word 'baste' and discuss the reasons for doing it.

Follow-up

During Rosh Hashanah, Jewish people send each other greetings cards. If possible, find some examples to show the children and then encourage them to design and make their own New Year cards.

Banana fudge

Festival: Hindu Festival of Diwali, late October to early November.

What you need
Ingredients: 1 large banana, 3 cardamom pods, 25g polyunsaturated margarine plus extra for greasing the tin, 50g semolina, 50g ground almonds, 50g brown sugar, 4 tablespoons water.
Equipment: a bowl, fork, polythene bag, rolling pin, saucepan, wooden spoon, hob, scales, tablespoon, shallow tin, fridge, 3 magnifying glasses, 6 small plates, greaseproof paper.

What to do
Peel the banana, break it into pieces into the bowl and mash it with the fork. Pop the cardamom pods, remove the seeds and put them into a polythene bag. Crush them by rolling the rolling pin over the bag then stir them into the mashed banana.

Melt the margarine in the saucepan, add the semolina and fry gently for 2 minutes. Remove from the hob and stir in the bananas, ground almonds, sugar and water. Mix thoroughly and then return to the heat. Bring to the boil and stir continuously until the mixture comes away from the sides of the saucepan. Grease the tin and pour the mixture into it. Spread evenly over the base of the tin and put it in the fridge to set for at least 2 hours. Cut into pieces and serve on the small plates.

Discussion
Diwali celebrates the New Year and the summer harvests. Talk about the festival and explain that sweetmeats, such as fudge and coconut barfi, are often made and given as gifts to relatives or taken to the temples. Lakshmi, the goddess of prosperity, is said to leave sweetmeats in those homes which are brightly lit by candles, fairy lights or traditional divas (clay lamps).

After the ingredients have been weighed, help the children to realise that the sugar, ground almonds and semolina all weigh the same. Look at each ingredient carefully to see if it looks like there is more of one than the others and talk about the reasons for this.

Look carefully at the cardamom pods using magnifying glasses. Does the smell remind the children of anything?

Compare the fudge mixture before and after chilling in the fridge. Does the colour, size, smell or texture change? As the children eat the fudge, make a list of as many words as possible to describe it — sticky, soft, slippery. Talk about the need to eat sweets in moderation and the importance of cleaning teeth to remove sugar.

Follow-up
Make paper doilies for the sweets. Draw around plates on to a piece of paper and cut out the circle. Show the children how to fold their circle into quarters and cut interesting shapes into the paper. Unfold the paper circle and use as a doily.

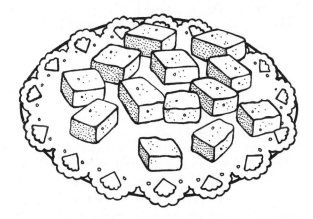

Karah Prashad

Festival: Baisakhi, Sikh New Year, 13 April.

What you need
Ingredients: 50g sugar, ½ litre water, 40g raisins, ½ tablespoon flaked almonds, 3 cardamom pods, 60g margarine, 60g semolina.
Equipment: scales, a measuring jug, tablespoon, plastic bag, rolling pin, saucepan, hob, wooden spoon, metal spoon, 6 small bowls, 6 spoons.

What to do
Dissolve the sugar in the water. Remove the seeds from the cardamom pods and stir into the sugared water. Crush the flaked almonds in the plastic bag with a rolling pin.

Heat the margarine in the saucepan and fry the semolina gently until it begins to brown. Stir in the sugared water, raisins and almonds. Heat gently until the semolina has softened. Stir frequently until all the liquid is absorbed.

Pour into 6 small bowls and serve.

Discussion
As well as marking the Sikh New Year, Baisakhi celebrates the founding of the Pure Sikh Community by Guru Gobind Singh. The festival lasts for three days and on the third day the congregation shares fruit and Karah Prashad.

Show the children the Karah Prashad at regular intervals and describe the changes as each ingredient is added. Talk about the correct position for the saucepan on the hob (with the handle facing inwards).

As the children eat the Karah Prashad, count the raisins in each bowl. Which child had most or least?

Follow-up
Guru Gobind Singh started the custom of all Sikh temples having a free kitchen where anyone can eat. To see whether this rule was being followed, he dressed as a traveller and knocked at many doors early in the morning. Each time he was turned away with a variety of excuses until he came to Bhai Nandlal's house where he was welcomed and given food. Act out this story.

Swedish Julgrot

Festival: Christmas, 25 December.

What you need
Ingredients: 750ml semi-skimmed milk, 25g polyunsaturated margarine and a little extra for greasing the dish, 75g short grain pudding rice, 25g sugar, 50g sultanas, 1 blanched almond.
Equipment: a measuring jug, scales, saucepan, wooden spoon, hob, heat-resistant mat, greaseproof paper, ovenproof dish, oven, 6 small bowls, 6 spoons.

What to do
Put the milk, rice and margarine into the saucepan. Bring to the boil then remove from the hob and place on a heat-resistant mat. Cool slightly and add the sugar, sultanas and almond and stir together.

Grease the ovenproof dish and pour the rice mixture into it. Bake in the oven at 200°C/400°F (Gas Mark 6) for 40 minutes until light brown on the top. Serve in the small bowls.

Discussion
In Sweden, this special rice pudding follows a traditional meal of dried salt cod, boiled potatoes and peas. One blanched almond is hidden in the pudding and the person who finds it in their dish will have good luck.

Can the children say whether the margarine comes from a plant or animal? Can they predict what will happen to the margarine when it is heated with the milk and rice? Encourage the children to describe what happens when the sugar is added. Does it dissolve or can it still be seen? Name other substances which dissolve (salt, stock cubes, jelly). Do they all need heat to dissolve?

Describe how the Julgrot changes after cooking. Compare the surface of the pudding with the inside. Discuss the importance of allowing the Julgrot to cool before eating. Who found the almond in their bowl?

Follow-up

In Sweden, Christmas is also a time for celebrating St Lucia (13 December). Many Swedish schools dress a child as St Lucia (white dress, red sash, crown of candles and evergreen branches) and have a procession around the school. Tell the story of St Lucia, act it out and make a frieze depicting the procession. (See *Bright Ideas for Early Years Festivals and Celebrations*, Scholastic.)

New Year cookies

Festival: Chinese New Year, between 21 January and 20 February.

What you need

Ingredients: 100g polyunsaturated margarine, 100g sugar, 25g raw peanuts, 1 tablespoon sesame seeds, 1 small egg, 175g rice flour, 50g cornflour.
Equipment: scales, a tablespoon, grill, grill pan, polythene bag, rolling pin, bowl, wooden spoon, oven, 2 baking trays, greaseproof paper, 6 small plates which can be put into pairs according to pattern.

What to do

Toast the sesame seeds under the grill until golden brown. Repeat with the peanuts and then place them in the polythene bag and crush them finely with the rolling pin. Cream the margarine with the sugar. Beat in the egg and fold in the flours. Stir in the peanuts and sesame seeds to make a stiff dough. Divide the dough into 12 balls and give 2 to each child. Flour the work surface to prevent the cookies sticking and ask each child to shape their ball into a circle (about 6cm in diameter and ½cm thick).

Line each baking tray with greaseproof paper. Place the cookies on the trays and bake in the oven at 180°C/ 350°F (Gas Mark 4) for 15 minutes. Share the cooked biscuits on to the 6 plates.

Discussion

During this festival, special symbolic foods are served to ensure good fortune. These include peanuts, melon seeds, preserved fruits, stuffed cakes and special biscuits such as New Year cookies.

Describe the changes in the peanuts and sesame seeds as they are grilled. Name other foods which are grilled. Compare the cookies before and after baking and describe any differences.

Talk about the patterns on the plates and match the pairs.

Follow-up

• It is customary at New Year for Chinese people to make sure their houses are thoroughly cleaned. They believe that Tsao Chun, the kitchen god, gives a report of the state of their houses to the God of Heaven. Link this to the importance of personal and kitchen hygiene.
• Continue matching patterns on plates by using photocopiable page 95. Decorate paper plates, cut them in half and use them for matching activities.

Dutch Sinterklaas biscuits

Festival: Christmas, St Nicholas' Eve, 5 December.

What you need

Ingredients: 100g polyunsaturated margarine, 50g sugar, 1 egg, 1 teaspoon cinnamon, 250g plain white flour, 1 teaspoon baking powder.

Equipment: scales, a teaspoon, bowl, wooden spoon, sieve, oven, 2 baking sheets, 6 knives, 6 forks, 6 spoons.

What to do

Put the margarine and sugar into the bowl and beat together with the wooden spoon. Beat in the egg and then stir in the cinnamon. Sieve the flour and baking powder into the bowl. Mix into a pastry-like dough and knead on a lightly floured surface until smooth.

Divide the dough into 6 pieces and ask each child to knead their dough for two or three minutes. Gently roll each piece of dough into a fat cylinder and cut it in half. Roll one piece of dough more thinly and ask each child to shape it into the initial for their first name. Try to make the letter in one piece but if breaking and joining is unavoidable. make sure the joins are firmly stuck.

Ask the children to use the other piece of dough to repeat the process, making the initial letter of their surname.

Decorate the biscuits with a texture or pattern by pressing knives, forks and spoons into the dough. Make these fairly deep otherwise they will be lost in the baking. Carefully place the letters on the baking sheets and cook in the oven at 200°C/400°F (Gas Mark 6) for 10 to 15 minutes until golden.

Discussion

In Holland, Christmas celebrations start on St Nicholas' Eve when a special Sinterklaas biscuit (made in the shape of each person's initial) marks each place at the table.

Look carefully at all the equipment you have used to make the biscuits and discuss the materials each item is made from. What are the advantages and disadvantages of each material?

Describe the effects of beating the sugar and margarine together. This is often called 'creaming'. Smell the cinnamon and name other familiar spices. Ask the children to describe the feel of the dough and suggest a reason for kneading it on a floured surface. Discuss the need for hygiene. What could happen if they were kneading the dough on a dirty surface?

Have any children got the same initials? Encourage them to use all parts of the tools to decorate their biscuits. which tools make dots, straight or curved lines?

Measure one of the biscuits before and after cooking by drawing round it. Describe any changes in size, colour and texture.

Follow-up

The Dutch have many interesting customs associated with St Nicholas' Eve which you could research. For example, each person in the family receives a 'joke' gift. Can the children design and make a 'joke' gift for someone in their own family?

Hot cross buns

Festival: Easter, late March to April.

What you need

Ingredients: 250g strong white flour, ½ teaspoon mixed spice, ½ teaspoon cinnamon, ½ teaspoon nutmeg, 25g polyunsaturated margarine plus extra for greasing the baking sheet, 25g sugar, 75g currants, ½ tablespoon easy blend dried yeast, 1 egg, 50ml water, 50ml milk. For the cross – 2 tablespoons flour, 2 tablespoons water.
Equipment: scales, a teaspoon, tablespoon, measuring jug, sieve, bowl, wooden spoon, kettle, warm place for proving, cling film, greaseproof paper, baking sheet, oven, 6 knives.

What to do

Put the milk into the measuring jug. Boil the kettle and add 50ml hot water to the milk. Leave the liquid to cool until it is hand hot. Sieve the flour and spices into the bowl. Rub in the margarine and then add the sugar, dried yeast and currants.

Beat the egg and stir into the dry ingredients. Gradually add the warm milk until a soft dough is produced. Knead the dough until smooth then return to the bowl, cover with cling film and leave to rise in a warm place for 30 minutes.

When risen, divide the dough into 6 pieces and ask each child to knead their own piece of dough. Shape into a bun and cut a cross into the top. Mix together the 2 tablespoons of flour with 2 tablespoons of water to make a paste then use a teaspoon to put the paste on to the cut cross. Grease the baking sheet and place the buns on to it. Leave to prove in a warm place for 30 minutes. Cook in the oven at 200°C/400°F (Gas Mark 6) for 10 minutes.

Discussion

The Christian fast of Lent was traditionally broken with hot cross buns on Good Friday. The cross represents the cross on which Jesus died. What other special foods do the children associate with Easter (Easter cakes and eggs)?

Identify which of the ingredients are the spices. Smell them and discuss the reason for including spices in foods. Warn the children not to touch their eyes after handling spices because some spices may cause irritation.

What will happen when the dough is left in a warm place? Which ingredient causes the dough to rise? When the buns are cooked, describe any changes that have taken place. Compare the bottom of the bun with the top. What has happened to the cross on the top?

Follow-up

Adapt the words of the rhyme '5 Currant Buns' (see below). Learn the rhyme and choose children to act as the characters (the 5 buns, the customer, the baker). Ask them to mime the actions as the rhyme is recited. Emphasise the subtraction involved in the rhyme — 5 buns take away 1 bun leaves 4 buns.

5 currant buns in the baker's shop,
Round and fat, with a cross on the top.
Along came a child with a penny one day,
Bought a currant bun and took it away.

4 currant buns in the baker's shop, etc.

Food from around the world

Chapter nine

Food is central to all cultures and offers an opportunity to develop children's awareness of the tremendous diversity of cultures. The traditional British diet of meat and two vegetables has been broadened considerably in recent years due to the influence of holidays abroad and improvements in transportation which make exotic foods easily available in many supermarkets. Multicultural recipes not only introduce children to an incredibly diverse range of ingredients, but can also be very nutritional as many are high in fibre, vitamins and minerals and low in fat and sugar.

Take advantage of any local contacts with people from other countries. Invite parents, grandparents or any other adult with different ethnic origins to talk to the children about food associated with their culture.

The following recipes are associated with particular countries and can be used to introduce children to food from abroad.

Tahini dip (Greece)

What you need
Ingredients: 4 tablespoons pale tahini, 2 tablespoons water, the juice of a lemon, 1 tablespoon sunflower oil, 2 teaspoons soy sauce, a range of raw vegetables and fruits to use with the dip (cauliflower, cucumber, tomatoes, celery, carrots, apple, radishes, parsley).
Equipment: a tablespoon, lemon squeezer, teaspoon, bowl, wooden spoon, 6 knives, 6 small plates, 6 spoons.

What to do
Put the tahini into the bowl and mix with the water. Blend to a smooth creamy sauce and then add the oil and soy sauce. Squeeze the lemon into the mixture. Stir together until the dip is smooth.

Wash and prepare the vegetables. Give each child a small plate and invite them to use the vegetables and fruits to make a picture of a flower garden (see Figure 1). Encourage them to cut, fold and bend the ingredients to create flowers, stems and leaves. More able children could be helped to cut flower shapes into the vegetables as suggested on page 26. When the children are satisfied with their picture, suggest they add a few spoonfuls of the tahini dip in appropriate places on their picture (as clouds, bushes, soil). Discuss the flower garden pictures before allowing the children to dip their fruit and vegetables into the tahini and eat them.

Discussion
Encourage the children to use all their senses to describe the tahini. Look on the ingredients label to find out what it is made from.

Describe the reaction of each ingredient as it is mixed into the dip. Does it float or sink? Does it mix easily with the other ingredients or does it tend to separate? How is the colour or texture of the dip altered? Talk about the taste of the dip. Does it remind them of anything else? Do they prefer their fruits and vegetables with or without the dip?

Vegetable and fruit pictures

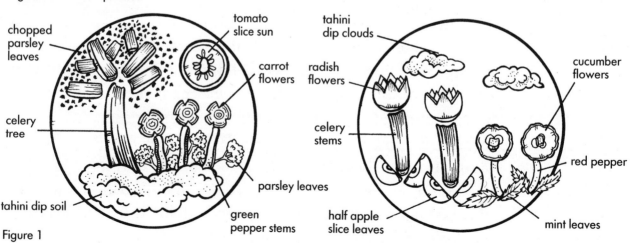

chopped parsley leaves

tomato slice sun

carrot flowers

celery tree

tahini dip soil

parsley leaves

green pepper stems

tahini dip clouds

radish flowers

celery stems

cucumber flowers

red pepper

half apple slice leaves

mint leaves

Figure 1

As the children design their flower pictures, talk with them about the importance of using a variety of shapes, colours and textures. Why do we need to make food look attractive?

Follow-up
● Locate Greece on a world map or globe.
● Find out about other Greek dips such as Hummus or Taramasalata. What are their ingredients? Make or buy some and have a tasting session.

Mint drink (called Podina Ka Sharbat – India)

What you need
Ingredients: 60g fresh mint, ½ teaspoon ground ginger, 100g sugar, 1 tablespoon lemon juice, 1200ml water, ice cubes, 6 mint leaves to decorate.
Equipment: scales, a teaspoon, tablespoon, food processor, 1 minute sand timer, sieve, 2 large jugs, 3 pestles and mortars (or bowls and wooden spoons), 3 polythene bags, 3 rolling pins, 6 glasses.

What to do
Wash the mint thoroughly and divide it between the three mortars. Ask the children to work in pairs (one holding the mortar and one using the pestle) to crush the leaves for a few minutes. Place all the mint into the food processor and blend for 2 minutes. Add the ground ginger, sugar, lemon juice and 600ml water and blend for 3 minutes.

Sieve the liquid into an empty jug to remove most of the mint leaves. Give each child a polythene bag and ask them to put 2 or 3 ice cubes into it. Twist the polythene bags round at the top to prevent the ice cubes coming out and use the rolling pin to tap the ice cubes to create crushed ice. Warn the children not to bang their fingers by mistake. Divide the mint drink among the 6 glasses and top up with the remaining water. Add a little crushed ice to each glass and a mint leaf for decoration.

Discussion
Look closely at the mint and name the parts of the plant (stem, leaves). Discuss the arrangement of the leaves along the stem and compare the number of leaves on two or three different stems. Smell the leaves before and after crushing and discuss when the smell is strongest. What happens to the colour of the leaves as they are crushed? Compare the methods of crushing the leaves by hand (using the pestle and mortar) and by machine.

Talk about the function of the sieve and ask the children to suggest other ways of separating liquids and solids.

Explore the ice cubes using all the senses and list words to describe them. Discuss why this drink is particularly suitable for people living in India and ask them to name drinks suitable for cold and hot climates.

Follow-up

Design a label for a bottle of this mint drink. Sketch out three or four different designs before choosing the most suitable one to make. Look at labels on other bottles of drink to discover what information is usually necessary — name of drink, name and address of manufacturer, ingredients, quantity, bar code and so on.

Tortillas (Mexico)

What you need

Ingredients: 125g plain white flour, ½ teaspoon salt, ½ teaspoon baking powder, 25g solid white vegetable or sunflower oil, water.
Equipment: scales, a teaspoon, bowl, frying pan, wooden spatula, hob, 3 rolling pins, 6 small plates, 6 knives, 6 forks.

What to do

Place the flour, salt and baking powder in the bowl. Rub in the solid vegetable oil until the mixture resembles fine breadcrumbs. Gradually add water until a soft dough is formed. Knead the dough on a floured surface until smooth. Leave to rest for 15 minutes.

Cut the dough into 6 pieces and give a piece to each child. Ask them to roll out the dough in a circle shape as thinly as possible on a lightly floured surface. Cook each tortilla separately in an ungreased frying pan for 2 minutes on each side until slightly brown but still soft. Press any bubbles down with the spatula. Serve each one on a small plate and, when cool enough, invite the children to eat them with their fingers or with a knife and fork. They could spread their tortillas with a paste, such as peanut butter, if they wish to give them extra flavour.

Discussion

Explain that tortillas are a type of bread and look at the ingredients you have used. Identify the missing ingredient (yeast) which would be used in making a traditional loaf. How is the bread different from our traditional loaves? If possible, have a loaf available for comparison. Explain that Mexicans eat tortillas in many different ways — plain, buttered, filled with meat and vegetables and rolled into pancakes.

Dry frying is an ancient traditional method of cooking because oils and fats were only introduced to Mexico by the Spanish invaders. Discuss the health advantages of dry frying.

Follow-up

Set up a baker's shop in the home corner. Look at a wide variety of breads and rolls, including examples from other cultures (French croissants, Indian chapattis, Italian grissini). Make pretend loaves and rolls from play dough, Plasticine, clay, papier mâché. Include signs, labels, posters, packaging, shopping lists and receipts. Visit a real baker's or the bakery section in a supermarket.

Dan-Dan noodles (China)

What you need

Ingredients: 180g thread egg noodles, 2 tablespoons sesame seed paste, 4 tablespoons water, 6 spring onions, a small piece of root ginger, 1 tablespoon soy sauce, 2 teaspoons vinegar, 900ml water, a vegetable stock cube.

Equipment: 3 saucepans (large, medium and small), scales, a tablespoon, grater, teaspoon, measuring jug, sieve, hob, 2 wooden spoons, 6 small bowls, 6 spoons, 6 knives, 6 forks, 6 pairs chopsticks.

What to do

Blend the sesame seed paste with the 4 tablespoons of water in the smallest saucepan. Chop the spring onions into small pieces and stir into the paste. Peel and grate the small piece of root ginger and stir into the paste. Add the soy sauce and vinegar and mix thoroughly. Warm the sauce on the hob, stirring frequently.

Put 900ml water into the middle-sized saucepan and add the stock cube. Bring to the boil and simmer for 2 minutes.

Fill the large saucepan with water and bring to the boil. Add the noodles and cook for 3 or 4 minutes until tender. Drain them in the sieve and share the noodles between the 6 small bowls. Put a spoonful of warm sauce on top of each bowl of noodles and then spoon the hot stock over the top.

Discussion

Place the saucepans in order of size from large to small and use them for work on capacity. How many small saucepans full of water will fill the large or medium-sized saucepan?

Smell the spring onions and root ginger before and after preparation. When is the smell strongest?

Explain that noodles are very popular in China and are often eaten at every meal. Look on the packet to find out the ingredients. Compare the cooked noodles with the original dried ones and describe the changes that have taken place. Offer each child a knife, fork, spoon and chopsticks. Ask them to find out the easiest way of eating the noodles.

Follow-up

Collect cooking equipment associated with Chinese cooking such as chopsticks, a wok, rice paddle, bamboo steamer. Use the equipment for observation drawings.

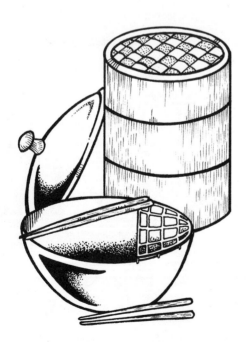

Minestrone soup (Italy)

What you need

Ingredients: 2 tablespoons olive oil, 1 onion, 1 potato, 2 carrots, 1 stem of celery, 75g cabbage, 4 or 5 canned tomatoes, vegetable stock cube, 900ml water, 1 bouquet garni sachet, 175g frozen peas, 50g tinned red kidney beans, 50g macaroni, black pepper, 50g Parmesan cheese.
Equipment: scales, a tablespoon, tin opener, measuring jug, grater, bowl, saucepan, wooden spoon, kettle, hob, 6 knives, 6 soup bowls, 6 spoons.

What to do

Skin and chop the onion finely. Peel and dice the potato and carrots. Chop the celery and cabbage finely. Put the tinned tomatoes into a bowl and chop into small pieces.

Heat the olive oil in the saucepan and fry the onion for 2 or 3 minutes until soft. Stir in the potato, carrots and celery and fry for 3 minutes. Add the cabbage and tomatoes and cook for 5 minutes.

Boil the kettle and pour hot water over the stock cube in the jug. When the cube has dissolved, add the stock and the bouquet garni sachet to the saucepan. Add the peas, kidney beans and macaroni and cover the saucepan.

Simmer gently for 15 minutes until the vegetables and pasta are tender. Season with black pepper and serve in the soup bowls. Grate the Parmesan cheese and sprinkle over the soup.

Discussion
Before preparing the vegetables, sort them into sets, for example, those which grow above or below the ground. Look for the veins on the cabbage and the celery and discuss their importance in taking water to every part of the plant.

Feel the macaroni and describe its appearance. Predict what will happen to it during cooking. What other types of pasta can the children name?

When the soup is served in the bowls, ask the children to look for solid shapes — cylinders, cubes, cuboids, spheres. How many different colours are there?

Follow-up
● Find other recipes for minestrone soup and compare the ingredients and methods used.
● Show how water is distributed throughout a plant by standing a stem of celery with a leafy top in a glass of coloured (use food colouring) water for one or two days.

Cheese soufflé (France)

What you need
Ingredients: 300ml semi-skimmed milk, 2 slices onion, 1 bay leaf, 1 parsley sprig, 40g polyunsaturated margarine plus a little extra for greasing the dish, 40g plain white flour, 50g Gruyère cheese, 4 eggs, a pinch of cayenne pepper.
Equipment: scales, a measuring jug, wooden spoon, metal spoon, soufflé dish, oven, grater, saucepan, hob, 3 bowls, 3 whisks, 6 knives, 6 small plates, 6 forks, greaseproof paper.

What to do
Chop the parsley and onion finely. Put the milk in the saucepan with the parsley, onion and bay leaf. Bring to the boil, remove from the heat and pour back into

the measuring jug. Leave to cool and allow the flavours to infuse. Remove the bay leaf before using the milk in the sauce.

Use a little margarine to grease the soufflé dish. Melt the 40g margarine in the saucepan and stir in the flour. Cook for 2 minutes and then gradually add the milk, stirring all the time. Bring to the boil and cook until the sauce is thick and even.

Grate the cheese and add it to the sauce. Stir until the cheese has melted. Remove the sauce from the heat and allow to cool slightly. Separate the eggs and stir in the egg yolks and a pinch of cayenne pepper. Ask the children to work in pairs to whisk the egg whites until stiff (one child holding the bowl, while the other uses the whisk). Fold the egg whites gently into the cheese sauce and spoon the mixture into the soufflé dish. Cook in the oven at 200°C/400°F (Gas Mark 6) for 25 minutes until well risen and golden brown. Serve on the small plates.

Discussion

Discuss the design of the egg carton. If possible, have several different designs available for comparison (boxes and trays, plastic and card, transparent and opaque). What are the advantages or disadvantages of each material? Which materials are environmentally friendly?

Show the children the sauce at regular intervals so they can observe the changes as the ingredients are added. Explain the term 'fold' and ask the children to give reasons for doing this gently. Predict what will happen to the soufflé. Why has it risen so much?

Follow-up

Talk about different cheeses. How many can the children name? Are they made in this country or do they come from abroad? Identify on a map the countries of origin of various cheeses such as Parmesan (Italy), Edam (Holland), Brie (France), feta (Greece) and have a tasting session.

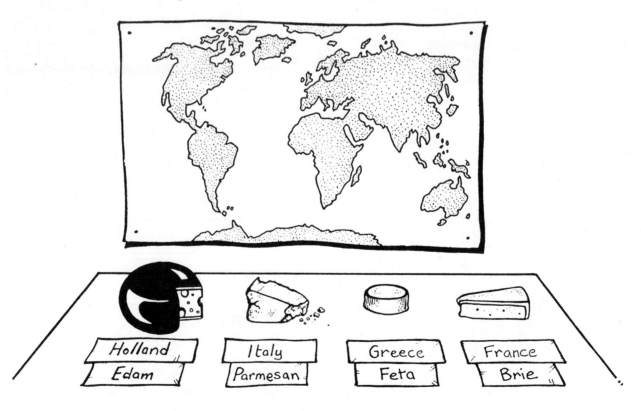

Food linked with stories

Chapter ten

Many traditional and well-known stories from different cultures centre on food and can be used as a stimulus for cookery activities, role-play and work in other areas. The stories in this chapter feature a range of different sorts of food and provide a wider context from which the children can see where our food comes from and the important role it plays in our life.

The recipes in this chapter are linked to popular stories used regularly with early years children. Many of the foods in traditional stories are no longer commonplace to children. For example, not all children have porridge for breakfast (Goldilocks and the Three Bears). Even more modern stories such as *Avocado Baby* by John Burningham sometimes centre on a food which many children may never have seen, let alone tasted. Making recipes based on the foods featured in these stories can bring another dimension to familiar, well-loved stories.

Each of the following recipes links with a popular story and although reference is made to a particular book, there are often many versions of the traditional stories. Similarly, there are many other stories for which recipes could be found and a list of these is given at the end of the chapter.

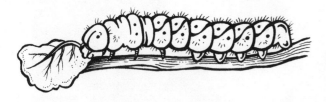

Caterpillar rolls

Story link: *The Very Hungry Caterpillar* by E. Carle, Picture Puffin.

What you need
Ingredients: 6 small bread finger rolls, ½ teaspoon green food colouring, 5 tablespoons water, 75g desiccated coconut, 6 tablespoons lime marmalade, 12 chocolate buttons, 12 strands All-bran, 250g golden marzipan.
Equipment: a bowl, teaspoon, metal spoon, scales, tablespoon, 6 knives, 6 small plates, 1 large plate.

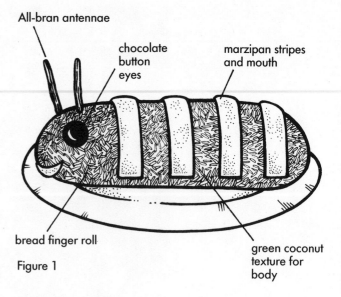

All-bran antennae

chocolate button eyes

marzipan stripes and mouth

bread finger roll

green coconut texture for body

Figure 1

What to do
Put the green food colouring, water and coconut into the bowl and mix until the coconut is evenly coloured. Spread the mixture out on the large plate. Ask each child to spread 1 tablespoon of lime marmalade on the top and sides of their finger roll. Press the roll into the coconut to cover the sides and ends and place on a small plate. Gently press 2 strands All-bran into one end of the roll for antennae. Use a little marmalade to stick on 2 chocolate button eyes. Divide the marzipan into 6 and use to make a mouth and stripes along the caterpillar's back (see Figure 1).

Discussion
Look at the packaging for each ingredient and compare the materials it is made from. Why does food need to be well packaged? Is anything overpackaged? Talk about recycling packaging, for example, making models or as containers for storing equipment.

Compare the feel of each ingredient and sort into sets such as dry, wet, sticky. Talk about the use of artificial food colourings to make food look more enticing and discuss the disadvantages of this.

As the children eat, talk about the purpose of the tongue (for moving food around and helping the process of swallowing). Look for taste buds and explain the need for saliva to moisten the food and aid digestion.

Follow-up
● Draw pictures of a different food for each day of the week. For example, one cake on Monday, two cabbages on Tuesday, three chips on Wednesday and so on. Punch holes in them and mount the drawings in a book. Use Blu-Tack to stick a picture of a caterpillar on to one of the foods. Move the caterpillar to a different food each day.
● Find out what real caterpillars eat.

Chocolate porridge

Story link: *Goldilocks and the Three Bears, Read it Yourself* series, Ladybird.

What you need
Ingredients: 175g porridge oats, 600ml water, 600ml semi-skimmed milk, 6 cubes cooking chocolate.
Equipment: scales, a measuring jug, saucer, saucepan, wooden spoon, hob, 3 graters, 6 small plates, 6 serving bowls, 6 spoons.

What to do
Put the milk and water into the saucepan. Add the porridge oats and bring to the boil on the hob. Simmer for 5 minutes, stirring all the time.

Give each child a plate and one cube of cooking chocolate. Suggest they work in pairs to grate their cube of chocolate on to their plate. It is easier if the children take turns to hold the grater over the plate and rub the chocolate up and down.

Serve the porridge in the bowls and ask each child to sprinkle their grated chocolate over the top. Remember to stand the saucepan on a heat resistant mat and warn the children that the saucepan will be hot even if it does not look it.

Discussion
Ask the children to describe the dry porridge oats. Predict what will happen when a pinch of oats is sprinkled on to the liquid in the saucepan. Do they float, sink, change colour?

What is the difference between 'boil' and 'simmer'? Why do we need to stir the porridge all the time? Listen as the porridge simmers and describe any noises.

Compare the grated chocolate before and after sprinkling on the porridge. What happens to the chocolate and what causes the change? What other substances melt when heated?

Follow-up
Play the Three Bears Breakfast Game. Photocopy page 96 and cut out the cards. The three players choose one of the cards showing the characters from the Three Bears story. Show them the other cards and talk about which ones they will need to collect for their character. For example, Daddy Bear will need the big bowl while Baby Bear will need the small place-mat. Turn the cards upside down and take turns to turn over a card. If it belongs to their character, they keep the card. If not, they return it upside down. The game finishes when one player has collected all the items for their character.

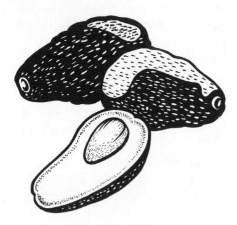

Avocado soup

Story link: *Avocado Baby* by John Burningham, Picture Lions.

What you need
Ingredients: 40g polyunsaturated margarine, ½ onion, 25g plain white flour, 600ml water, vegetable stock cube, 1 large ripe avocado, 2 teaspoons lemon juice, black pepper, 300ml semi-skimmed milk.
Equipment: scales, a measuring jug, teaspoon, saucepan, kettle, hob, bowl, sieve, 1 minute sand timer, 6 knives, 6 small soup bowls and 6 spoons.

What to do
Skin the onion and chop finely. Melt the margarine in the saucepan and fry the onion gently for about 3 minutes until soft. Stir in the flour and cook for about 1 minute.

Boil the water, pour into the measuring jug and dissolve the stock cube in it. Gradually add the stock to the flour and onion mixture and bring to the boil.

Peel the avocado, remove the stone and chop the flesh into small pieces. Add to the soup with the lemon juice and a pinch of pepper. Cover and simmer for 10 minutes.

Allow the soup to cool slightly and then sieve into a bowl. Stir in the milk and then return the soup to the saucepan. Warm through and then serve in the soup bowls.

Discussion
Look at the margarine at different stages of melting and describe what is happening. Use the sand timer to time cooking the onions and flour.

Which part of the plant is the avocado? Contrast the outside of the avocado with the inside. Feel the large stone and describe it. Taste a small piece of the raw avocado.

When washing up the equipment, try using plain water first. Look on the surface of the water for oil and feel the equipment. Then add some washing-up liquid and observe the difference.

Follow-up
Many foods like avocado turn brown when cut and exposed to the air. Lemon juice is used to combat this effect. Set up some experiments to observe what happens to a range of foods when exposed to the air and compare this to samples coated in lemon juice. Try small pieces of avocado, apple, pear, banana, potato and carrot.

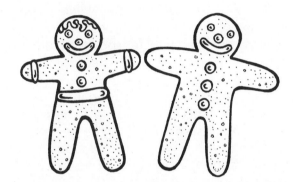

Gingerbread biscuits

Story link: *The Gingerbread Man, Read it Yourself* series, Ladybird.

What you need
Ingredients: 2 tablespoons clear honey, 1 tablespoon golden syrup, 25g polyunsaturated margarine, 175g plain wholemeal flour, ½ teaspoon bicarbonate of soda, 1 teaspoon cold water, 2 teaspoons ground ginger, 1 egg yolk, small quantity of ready-to-use icing for decoration.
Equipment: scales, a tablespoon, teaspoon, bowl, wooden spoon, saucepan, rolling pin, hob, gingerbread man pastry cutter, oven, large plate for serving, 2 baking sheets.

What to do
Put the honey, syrup and margarine into the saucepan and heat gently until melted.

Put the flour, ground ginger and egg yolk into the bowl and stir in the honey mixture. Mix the bicarbonate of soda with the cold water and add to the mixture.

Knead the dough on a lightly floured surface until smooth. Roll the dough out thinly and use the pastry cutter to cut out one or two gingerbread men for each child. Place the gingerbread men on two lightly floured baking sheets and cook in the oven at 180°C/350°F (Gas Mark 4) for 10 minutes.

Allow the gingerbread men to cool and then share them out to the children. Give each child a little ready-to-use icing and suggest they use it to decorate their gingerbread man, adding features (eyes, nose, mouth, hair) and simple items of clothing (belt, buttons, tie, braces) — see Figure 1. Make a circle of gingerbread men on the large plate.

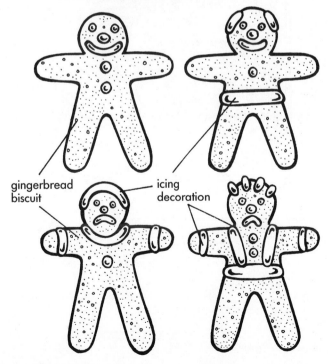

gingerbread biscuit

icing decoration

Figure 1

Discussion

Which ingredients contain sugar? Why should we take care with the amount of sugar we eat?

Talk about the changes which occur to the honey, syrup and margarine as they are heated. How does the honey mixture change the dry ingredients? Explain the purpose of the bicarbonate of soda and ask the children to name other ingredients or methods which are used to put air into food.

Name parts of the body on the gingerbread men. Estimate how many gingerbread men will fit on to one baking sheet. Describe the gingerbread men before and after cooking.

Follow-up

Find out about teeth. What function do teeth perform? Discuss tooth decay and make a chart to show which foods are 'good' and 'bad' for teeth.

Savoury pancake

Story link: *The Big Pancake* by Vera Southgate, Ladybird.

What you need

Ingredients: 125 self-raising wholemeal flour, 1 egg, 300ml semi-skimmed milk, 1 tablespoon sunflower oil plus a little extra for frying, 1 onion, 6 tomatoes, 125g frozen green beans, 1 teaspoon mixed herbs, black pepper, 100g Cheddar cheese, 6 sprigs of parsley.
Equipment: scales, a measuring jug, tablespoon, teaspoon, small dish, frying pan, wooden spatula, grater, kettle, large ovenproof dish, oven, hob, saucepan, wooden spoon, 2 bowls, 6 plates, 6 knives, 6 spoons, 6 forks.

What to do

Put the tomatoes into a bowl and pour hot water over the top – *this must be done by an adult.* Leave for a few minutes to cool and then remove them from the bowl. Skin the tomatoes, chop the flesh and place in the saucepan. Chop the onion finely and add to the saucepan with the green beans, mixed herbs and pepper. Bring to the boil, cover and simmer for 10 minutes. This is the pancake filling.

Put the flour into a bowl and stir in the egg. Gradually stir in the milk and the oil. Beat thoroughly until smooth. Heat a few drops of oil in the frying pan and add 3 spoonfuls of pancake mixture. Tilt the frying pan to spread the pancake mixture thinly over the bottom of the pan. Cook until the underside of the pancake is brown and then turn over and cook the other side. There should be enough mixture to make 6 pancakes.

Grate the cheese and place into the small dish. Give each child a plate and turn their pancake on to it. Ask each child to put 2 to 3 spoonfuls of filling along the middle of their pancake and sprinkle a little grated cheese over the top. Roll up the pancake and place it in the ovenproof dish. When all the pancakes are in the dish, sprinkle any remaining cheese over the top and cook in the oven at 180°C/350°F (Gas Mark 4) for 10 minutes until golden.

Give each child a sprig of parsley and ask them to chop it finely. When the pancakes are cooked, put one on each plate and sprinkle the parsley on top.

Discussion

Contrast the feel of the tomatoes after they have been in hot water and after they have been skinned. Why put the tomatoes into hot water first?

Touch the frozen green beans and compare how they feel with the warm tomatoes. Leave one or two beans to one side and time how long it takes them to thaw completely. Describe the smell as the filling is cooking.

Add the oil to the milk before stirring into the flour to see whether the oil floats or sinks. Which is lightest — the oil or the milk? Explain that hot oil or fat can sometimes catch fire and discuss the correct way of dealing with it (never use water, smother with the saucepan lid or a fire blanket). Advise the children to seek help immediately. Talk about the safety equipment in the cookery area.

Follow-up

● Learn this traditional rhyme about a pancake:

Mix a pancake,
Stir a pancake,
Pop it in the pan.
Fry a pancake,
Toss a pancake,
Catch it if you can!

● Design a place-mat. Will it be a rectangle or a circular pancake shape? What materials will the children use (card, fabric, thread)? How could they make their place-mat easy to clean?

Pastry lunchbaskets

Story link: *The Lighthouse Keeper's Lunch* by Ronda and David Armitage, Picture Puffin.

What you need

Ingredients: 300g white self-raising flour, 75g polyunsaturated margarine, 75g solid sunflower oil, 227g cream cheese, 4 tablespoons yoghurt, 3 slices cucumber, 3 slices red pepper, ½ carrot.

Equipment: scales, a tablespoon, sieve, rolling pin, 6cm and 8cm circle-shaped cutters, baking sheet, oven, wooden spoon, greaseproof paper, 2 bowls, 6 knives, 6 forks, 6 small plates.

What to do

Sieve the flour into the bowl. Rub in the margarine and fat until the mixture resembles fine breadcrumbs. Add enough water to mix into a dough.

Cut the dough in half. Roll out one half until roughly ½cm thick. Use the 8cm cutter to cut out 6 circles for the base of the baskets. Roll out the other piece of dough until roughly 2cm thick. Use the 8cm cutter to cut out 6 circles then use the 6cm cutter to cut a hole in each large circle. Rub a little water around the edge of the base circles and press one ring gently on to each base (see Figure 1).

Grease the baking sheet and place the baskets on the sheet. For the handles, roll out cylinder shapes of dough roughly 10cm long, shape them into a curve to fit the basket and lie them flat on the baking sheet. Cook in the oven at 200°C/400°F (Gas Mark 6) for 20 minutes.

Remove the baskets from the oven and allow to cool. Mix the cream cheese and yoghurt together. Put one tablespoon of this mixture into each basket. Cut the cucumber, red pepper and carrot into small pieces and push into the cream cheese to decorate. Gently press a pastry handle into each basket.

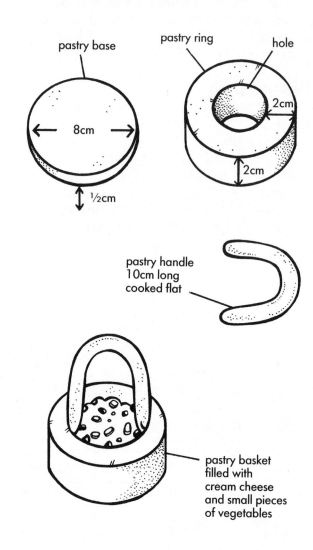

Figure 1

Discussion

Explain that the children are going to make a pastry basket like the one used to carry the lighthouse keeper's lunch. This pastry contains two types of fat. Identify them and name other foods which contain fat. Discuss the disadvantages of diets which include lots of high fat foods.

Feel and describe the greaseproof paper. How does it change when it has been used to rub fat on to the baking sheet? Try rubbing margarine on other types of paper and describe the changes you can see.

Compare the pastry baskets before and after cooking and describe any changes.

Follow-up

● Make up the contents of the lighthouse keeper's lunchbasket. Draw suggestions on a zig-zag book shaped like a basket.
● Investigate containers for carrying food. Compare the design of the basket used by Mrs Grinling with plastic lunchboxes. Discuss the advantages and disadvantages of each. Challenge older children to design and make a seagull-proof lunch container.

Animal rolls

Story link: *The Little Red Hen* by Margot Zemach, Hutchinson.

What you need

Ingredients: 250g wholemeal flour, ½ teaspoon castor sugar, ½ teaspoon salt, 15g polyunsaturated margarine plus a

little extra for spreading on the finished rolls, 1 teaspoon easy-blend dried yeast, 150ml warm water, 1 egg, currants for decoration.
Equipment: scales, a teaspoon, measuring jug, sieve, baking sheet, bowl, oven, a warm place for proving, jug, fork, pastry brush, cling film, 6 knives, 6 small plates for serving.

What to do

Sieve the flour into the bowl. Add the sugar and salt and rub in the margarine until the mixture resembles breadcrumbs. Stir in the yeast and water and mix to a soft dough. Knead lightly on a floured surface for about 5 minutes. Return to the bowl and cover with cling film. Leave in a warm place for 10 minutes.

Divide the dough into 6 pieces and give each child a piece. Ask them to knead their dough again for 3 minutes and then shape it into any animal of their choice. Talk about which animal shapes would be most suitable — rounded ones without long thin legs, for example snakes, worms, caterpillars, hedgehogs, ladybirds. Encourage the children to make their shapes by pinching or pulling the dough outwards rather than by trying to stick pieces together. If appropriate, suggest they use their knives or other utensils to draw lines on to their creature.

Place the animals on a floured baking sheet, cover with cling film and leave to rise in a warm place for 15 minutes. Beat the egg and then brush it over each animal. Allow the children to use currants to add features such as eyes or spots (see Figure 1).

Bake in the oven at 220°C/425°F (Gas Mark 7) for 15 minutes until golden. Allow the children to choose whether to cut their animal roll in half and spread it with margarine or to eat it as it is.

Discussion

Predict what will happen when the dough is left in a warm place. Leave a small piece in the fridge for comparison. What effect will the beaten egg have on the rolls?

Contrast the rolls before and after cooking, identifying any changes caused by heating. Tap the base of each roll with a spoon and describe the sound.

Which are the best animal shapes? How could any less successful designs be improved next time?

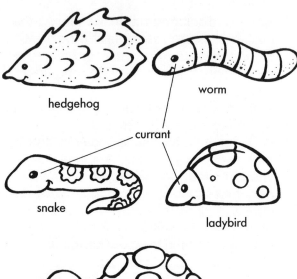

hedgehog

worm

currant

snake

ladybird

tortoise

Figure 1

Follow-up

Compare fresh yeast and dried yeast. Describe their feel, smell and appearance. Do the children realise that yeast is a fungus? To demonstrate the release of carbon dioxide bubbles which make the dough rise, mix a little of the fresh yeast with tepid water and a little sugar. Keep the yeast liquid warm and watch what happens. Put some of the liquid into a fridge as a comparison. (The liquid in the fridge will have fewer bubbles.)

Stuffed turnips

Story link: *The Enormous Turnip (Read It Yourself* series, Ladybird Books).

What you need

Ingredients: 3 turnips, 25g Cheddar cheese, 50g wholemeal bread, 150ml semi-skimmed milk, ½ onion, 25g polyunsaturated margarine, a vegetable stock cube, 300ml water, ½ teaspoon dried thyme, 1 egg.
Equipment: scales, a bread knife, vegetable knife, grapefruit knife, measuring jug, saucepan, wooden spoon, kettle, teaspoon, bowl, fork, tablespoon, hob and oven, casserole dish with lid, grater, greaseproof paper, 6 small plates, 6 knives and 6 forks.

What to do

Chop the bread into small pieces and soak it in the milk in a bowl for half an hour. Peel the turnips and cut them in half. Use the grapefruit knife to scoop out a slight hollow in each turnip half (an adult will probably need to do this).

Skin the onion and chop finely. Melt the margarine in a saucepan and fry the onion gently until cooked.

Crumble the vegetable stock cube in the jug, boil the water in the kettle and pour over the cube. Stir until the cube has dissolved.

Grease the casserole dish with margarine. Mash the soaked bread with a fork and stir in the cooked onion, the thyme and the egg. Put two or three tablespoons of the bread mixture into the hollow in each turnip. Place the stuffed turnips into the casserole dish and add the vegetable stock. Grate the cheese and sprinkle it over the bread stuffing.

Put the lid on the casserole dish and bake in the oven 220°C/425°F (Gas Mark 7) for 50 minutes. Serve each child with half a turnip on a small plate.

Discussion

What happens when the bread is placed into the milk? What other foods or materials absorb liquids?

Which part of the turnip plant will the children eat? Can they name other root vegetables? Taste and describe the raw turnip flesh that is scooped out from the hollow. As the children eat the cooked turnips, talk about the changes that have taken place. How have they changed in colour and texture? What has happened to the cheese?

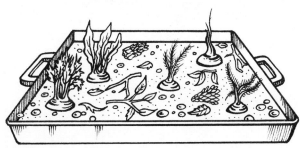

Follow-up

Save the root tops from the turnips and make a collection of the tops from a wide range of root vegetables. Place them in a shallow container with a little water and watch to see if new leaves grow. Turn the sprouting root tops into a miniature garden or landscape by adding other natural materials such as stones, fir cones, leaves, twigs and so on.

Further reading

The following stories also involve food and could initiate cookery sessions.

Meg's Eggs and *Meg's Veg* Helen Nicoll and Jan Pienkowski (Picture Puffin).
The Giant Jam Sandwich John Vernon Lord (Piper Picture Books).
Teddy Bear Baker Phoebe and Selby Worthington (Picture Puffin).
Mr. Ginger's Potato Sheila Lavelle (A&C Black).
The Magic Pasta Pot Tomie de Paola (Methuen).
Benny Bakes a Cake Eve Rice (Bodley Head).
The Doorbell Rang Pat Hutchins (Bodley Head).
The Magic Porridge Pot Paul Galdone (Heinemann).
The Old Woman and the Rice Thief Betsy Bang and Molly Garrett Bang (Hamish Hamilton).
The Shopping Basket John Burningham (Cape).
The Grape That Ran Away William Stobbs (Bodley Head).
Mr Bingle's Apple Pie Anne Wellington and Niki Sowter (Abelard).
The Tale of Mucky Mabel J. Willis and M. Chamberlain (Andersen Press).
The Baked Bean Queen John Burningham (Picture Lions).
Having a Picnic Sarah Garland (Picture Puffin).
The Witch in the Cherry Tree Margaret Mahy (Picture Puffin).
Apple Pigs Ruth Orbach (Picture Lions).

Some of these titles may now be out of print. Try libraries.

Bubbly toast, see page 22

Where does this food come from?

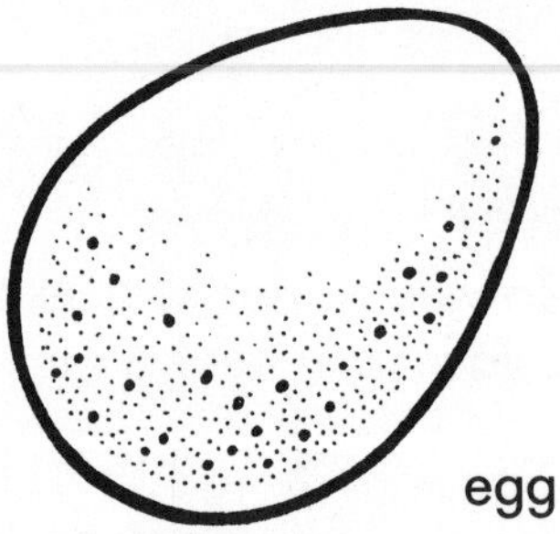

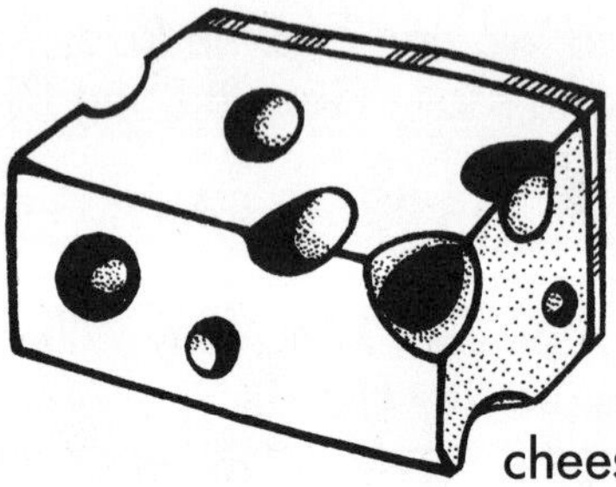

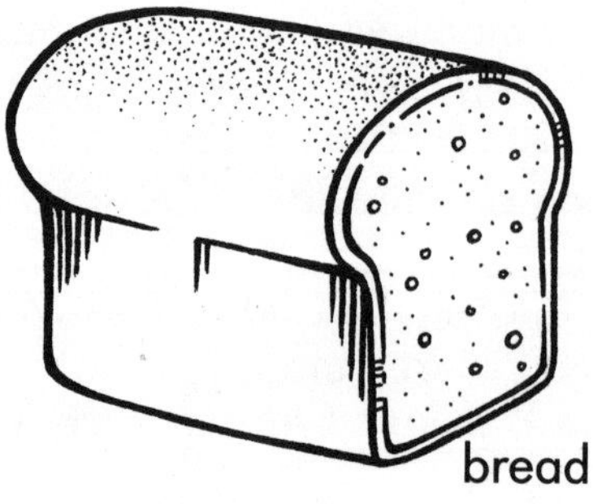

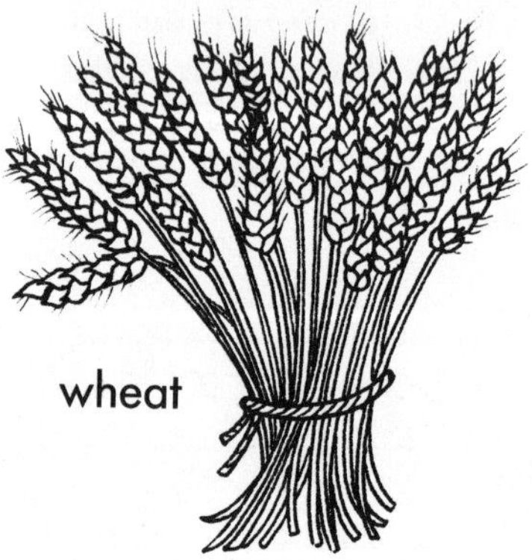

egg

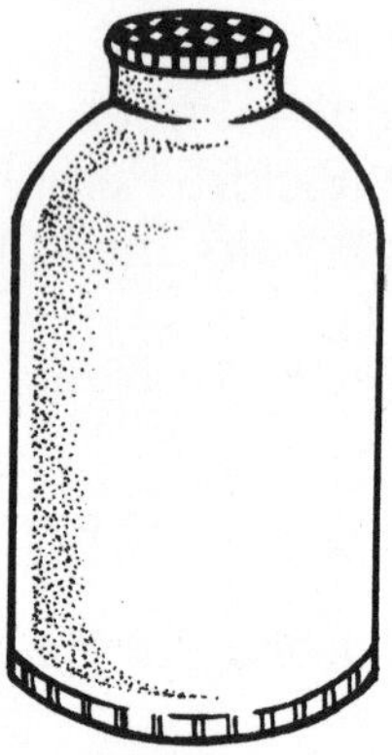

cow

milk

chicken

cheese

wheat

bread

Fruit salad, see page 42

Outside　　　　　　　　　　　**Inside**

Hot chocolate, see page 59

Design a party straw

Think of some ideas and draw them in the boxes below.

First idea	Second idea	Third idea

Tick the one you want to make.

Draw what you will need.

Now try to make it.

New Year cookies, see page 69

Match the broken plates.
Colour both pieces of each plate the same colour.

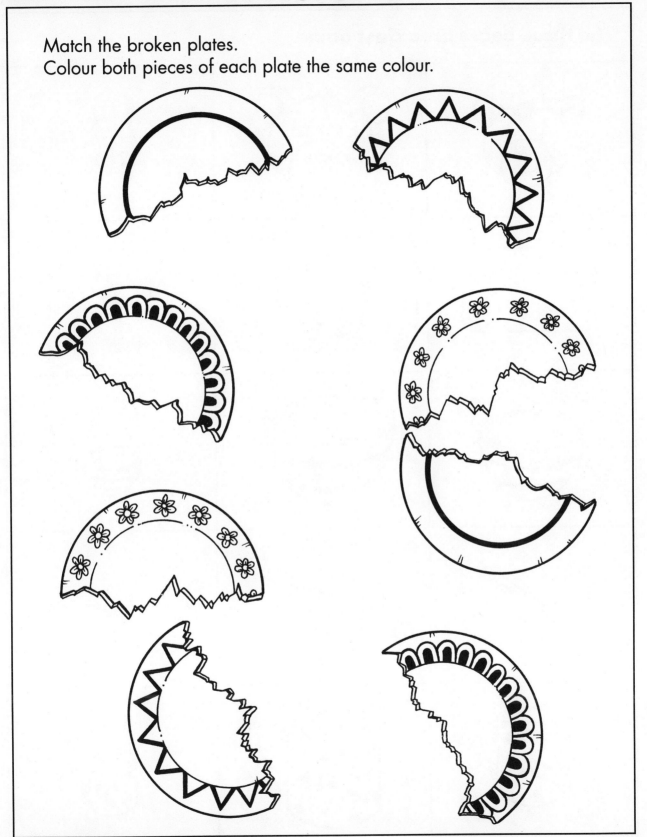

Chocolate porridge, see page 83

The three bears breakfast game

This page may be photocopied for use in the classroom and should not be declared in any return in respect of any photocopying licence.